Environmental Performance Auditing in the Public Sector

Environment and sustainable development challenges are a matter of global concern. Trillions of dollars of mostly public money are invested every year in domestic and international policies and programmes to address these challenges. The effectiveness of these policies and programmes is critical to environmental sustainability. Performance audits that examine the effectiveness of governmental policies and programmes heavily influence their implementation. Despite this, performance auditing in the environment field has received very little academic attention.

This book takes a closer look at performance auditing of public sector environmental policies and programmes. It examines trends in global environmental performance auditing and also how it is currently practised, drawing on a global survey and case studies from Canada, India and Australia. In doing so, it identifies issues and challenges faced by Supreme Audit Institutions in undertaking these performance audits.

This book will be of interest to students, scholars and practitioners of sustainable development, environmental auditing and public sector auditing as well as to donor organizations engaged in these areas.

Dr. Awadhesh Prasad is a visiting fellow at the Australian National University's Fenner School of Environment and Society, and works at the Murray-Darling Basin Authority, Australia, where he has been involved in monitoring and auditing of environmental policies and programmes for over 15 years.

Routledge Explorations in Environmental Studies
www.routledge.com/Routledge-Explorations-in-Environmental-Studies/book-series/REES

The Governance of Green Urban Spaces in the EU
Social innovation and civil society
Judith Schicklinski

NGO Discourses in the Debate on Genetically Modified Crops
Ksenia Gerasimova

Sustainability in the Gulf
Challenges and Opportunities
Edited by Elie Azar and Mohamed Abdelraouf

Environmental Human Rights
A Political Theory Perspective
Edited by Markku Oksanen, Ashley Dodsworth and Selina O'Doherty

African Philosophy and Environmental Conservation
Jonathan O. Chimakonam

Domestic Environmental Labour
An Eco-feminist Perspective on Making Homes Greener
Carol Farbotko

Stranded Assets and the Environment
Risk, resilience and opportunity
Edited by Ben Caldecott

Society, Environment and Human Security in the Arctic Barents Region
Edited by Kamrul Hossain and Dorothée Cambou

Environmental Performance Auditing in the Public Sector
Enabling Sustainable Development
Awadhesh Prasad

Environmental Performance Auditing in the Public Sector

Enabling Sustainable Development

Awadhesh Prasad

Routledge
Taylor & Francis Group
LONDON AND NEW YORK

earthscan
from Routledge

First published 2018 by Routledge

2 Park Square, Milton Park, Abingdon, Oxfordshire OX14 4RN
52 Vanderbilt Avenue, New York, NY 10017

Routledge is an imprint of the Taylor & Francis Group, an informa business

First issued in paperback 2019

British Library Cataloguing-in-Publication Data
A catalogue record for this book is available from the British Library

Library of Congress Cataloging-in-Publication Data
Names: Prasad, Awadhesh, author.
Title: Environmental performance auditing in the public sector : enabling sustainable development / Awadhesh Prasad.
Description: Abingdon, Oxon ; New York, NY : Routledge, 2018. |
Series: Routledge explorations in environmental studies |
Includes bibliographical references and index.
Identifiers: LCCN 2018004022 (print) | LCCN 2018019253 (ebook) |
ISBN 9781351273480 (eBook) | ISBN 9781138574625 (hardback)
Subjects: LCSH: Environmental auditing. | Environmental policy–Evaluation. |
Sustainable development–Government policy. Classification: LCC TD194.7 (ebook) |
LCC TD194.7 .P73 2018 (print) | DDC 333.7–dc23
LC record available at https://lccn.loc.gov/2018004022

ISBN: 978-1-138-57462-5 (hbk)
ISBN: 978-0-367-85604-5 (pbk)

Typeset in Goudy
by Out of House Publishing

Contents

Figures

Tables

Acknowledgements

The book is primarily based upon my doctoral dissertation, accepted by the Australian National University (ANU) in 2017. I am grateful to my supervisors, Prof. Stephen Dovers and Prof. Karen Hussey, for their valuable suggestions, guidance and encouragement during the study. I am particularly thankful to Steve for his encouragement to write this book and for reviewing the manuscript. I also wish to thank the two retired Auditors General of Australia – Messrs Pat Barrett and Ian McPhee – for sharing their accumulated knowledge and wisdom and providing comments and suggestions during my research at ANU. Ian was instrumental in getting the Working Group on Environmental Auditing (WGEA) Secretariat at the Audit Board of Indonesia to agree to organizing the global survey of Auditors General for my research. Further, I am also grateful to Pat and Ian for their review of the manuscript.

I would like to thank Messrs Mark Simpson and Grant Caine and Ms Deborah Jackson of the Australian National Audit Office (ANAO) for their help with the research related to the ANAO. Ms Tamie Plant of the ANAO gets my thanks for following up with the WGEA Secretariat for the survey. I would also like to thank Ms Atoorva Sinha and Mr Subhas Pandey from the office of the Comptroller and Auditor General (CAG) of India for their help with information on the operations of the CAG. I would also like to thank Ms Kimberly Leach and Mr George Stuetz of the Office of the Auditor General (OAG) of Canada for providing information on the operations of the OAG.

I wish to thank the WGEA Secretariat and especially Ms Ami Rahmawati for organizing the survey for my research. In addition to this survey, the WGEA has been a key source of data and information for my research, including the data on environmental audits, WGEA surveys and all environmental performance audit reports of Australia, Canada and India. I sincerely acknowledge the WGEA as a key source of data and information. I also wish to thank all audit offices across the globe, who through their kind participation in the survey, made an invaluable contribution to my research. Further, I wish to acknowledge the ANAO and the *International Journal of Government Auditing* for their permission to reproduce certain copyright materials in this book.

My special thanks go to my friend Mr Anil Dhir, who built the database of environmental audits and provided immense help with data analysis. Finally, and most importantly, I would like to thank my wife, Kavita, and daughters, Neeharika and Snigdha, for their continual understanding, love and support that enabled me to complete this challenging journey spanning a thesis and a book.

Awadhesh Prasad
Canberra
January 2018

Abbreviations

ADB	Asian Development Bank
AFROSAI	African Organization of Supreme Audit Institutions
ANAO	Australian National Audit Office
ARABOSAI	Arab Organization of Supreme Audit Institutions
ASAE	Australian Standards for Assurance Engagement
ASOSAI	Asian Organization of Supreme Audit Institutions
AUASB	Auditing and Assurance Board of Australia
BPG	better practice guides
CAG	Comptroller and Auditor General of India
CAROSAI	Caribbean Organization of Supreme Audit Institutions
CESD	Commissioner of Environment and Sustainable Development
CPA	Chartered Professional Accountants
CPIA	Country Policy and Institutional Assessment
CSO	civil society organization
EA	environmental agency
EIA	environmental impact assessment
EMS	environmental management system
EPA	environmental performance audit
EUROSAI	European Organization of Supreme Audit Institutions
GAO	Government Accountability Office, United States of America
GDP	gross domestic product
GFC	global financial crisis
GNI	gross national income
ICC	International Chamber of Commerce
iCED	International Centre for Environment Audit and Sustainable Development
IDI	INTOSAI Development Initiative
INCOSAI	International Congress of Supreme Audit Institutions
INTOSAI	International Organization of Supreme Audit Institutions
IRAI	International Development Association Resource Allocation Index
ISSAI	International Standards of Supreme Audit Institutions
ISO	International Organisation for Standardisation

JCPAA	Joint Committee on Public Accounts and Audit
KPI	key performance indicators
MDGs	Millennium Development Goals
MEAs	multilateral environmental agreements
NAO	National Audit Office of the United Kingdom
NGO	non-governmental organization
NRC	Natural Resource Commission
NPM	new public management
NRM	natural resource management
OAG	Office of the Auditor General of Canada
OECD	Organization for Economic Co-operation and Development
OLACEFS	Organization of Latin American and Caribbean Supreme Audit Institutions
OPP	One Pass Planning
PAC	public account committee
PASAI	Pacific Association of Supreme Audit Institutions
QMF	quality management framework
SAI	Supreme Audit Institution (the Highest Public Audit Office of a Country)
SAP	strategic audit plan
SDGs	sustainable development goals
SOE	state of environment
UN	United Nations
UNDP	United Nations Development Programme
UNEP	United Nations Environment Programme
UNESCO	United Nations Educational, Scientific and Cultural Organization
WGEA	INTOSAI Working Group on Environmental Auditing
WSSD	World Summit on Sustainable Development

1 Introduction

Background

Due to drivers such as population growth, industrialization, globalization and the digital revolution, the world is changing very rapidly, both in its natural and socio-political domains. Impending exceedance of some critical thresholds in the natural domain will likely adversely affect life-support functions of the earth, with significant adverse implications for human well-being (UNEP 2012: 6). One such consequence, climate change induced by global warming, is already being felt. The three recent consecutive years – 2015, 2016 and 2017 – have all been in 'the top three years in terms of temperature records' (Taalas, 2017). Governments across the world have been endeavouring to combat such environmental challenges through both domestic and international actions. Such environmental policy initiatives have been taken at least since the 1960s (Keene and Pullin, 2011), when visible environmental degradation and consequent public pressure for environmental protection (Chertow and Esty, 1997; Durant et al., 2004; Fiorino, 2001) prompted policy interventions by governments the world over – both nationally and internationally. More than 300 multilateral environmental agreements (MEAs) are currently operating to address global environmental challenges (e.g. loss of biodiversity, climate change). 'Environmental protection and sustainable development are among the most topical issues that face governments in the new millennium' (INCOSAI, 2010). Globally, trillions of dollars of mostly public money are invested every year in domestic and international programmes to maintain and enhance environmental quality. The effectiveness of these programmes is critical to environmental sustainability. The effectiveness of governments' programmes is examined through evaluations undertaken mostly by the private sector and through performance audits undertaken by independent Auditors General, also known as Supreme Audit Institutions (SAIs.)[1] Evaluation and performance auditing are similar in aims, approaches, analytical methodologies and techniques (Barrett, 2001; Pollitt and Summa, 1996). However, compared with the former, the latter has scarcely been studied in the environmental field. This is the focus of this book.

Environmental audits undertaken by SAIs can and do play a crucial role in the implementation of environmental initiatives, including those in MEAs (UNEP,

2010: iii) aimed at environmental protection and sustainable development. These audits, particularly environmental performance audits, that SAIs have been undertaking for over two decades, have resulted in governments' actions both domestically and internationally to improve environmental sustainability (WGEA, 2012).

Sustainable development and the role of SAIs

The concept of 'development that meets the needs of the present generation without compromising the ability for future generations to meet their own needs' (WCED, 1987) was put forward in the late 1980s. Over the years, the concept has become so comprehensive and complex that it is assumed to encompass all that is good and desirable (Holden et al., 2014). A large literature on sustainable development has developed (see Holden et.al., 2014 for a concise review), with sometimes divergent views – a review of which is beyond the scope of this book. Suffice it to say that gradually the concept has gained acceptance and currency in both the public and private sectors. It is now a major consideration in government planning and policy making (WGEA, 2007a: 15). About one-quarter of SAIs reported in the fifth survey (WGEA, 2007a: 15) that they were conducting audits of sustainable development programmes.

Building upon the earlier initiatives toward sustainable development – such as Agenda 21, reached at the Rio Earth Summit, 1992; the UN Millennium Development Goals (MDGs), 2000; World Summit on Sustainable Development (WSSD), 2002; and the Rio+20 Summit in 2012 – world leaders unanimously adopted new sustainable development goals (SDGs) in September 2015. This was immediately followed up by another landmark agreement on climate change at the Paris climate conference in December 2015. Together with the Paris Climate Agreement, the SDGs (17 goals, 169 targets) set the agenda for governmental efforts across the world for sustainable development for decades to come: to end poverty, fight inequality and injustice, and tackle climate change by 2030 (UNDP, 2016). SDGs are a complex web of integrated and interdependent global priorities that need effective governance systems, institutions, partnerships and intellectual and financial resources for their effective, efficient and coherent implementation (ICSU, 2017). The UN Division for Sustainable Development (UN-DSD, 2017) through the High-level Political Forum and Sustainable Development Knowledge Platform, among other means, provides leadership to the implementation of SDGs.

Good governance within each country and at the international level is essential for sustainable development (UN-WSSD, 2002). Topfer (2004) observes that 'sustainable development cannot be achieved without good governance, and good governance, in turn, is greatly furthered by the valuable work of SAIs. Therefore, SAIs can play a vital role in informing and supporting efforts to achieve sustainable development.' Due to their independence, SAIs are in a unique position 'to legitimately and credibly evaluate the efficiency and effectiveness of government policy and obligations' (Topfer, 2004). SAIs are critical to protecting the use of public finances for sustainable development. By providing crucial information on the use and management of public resources, they contribute to transparency and accountability of the public administration for these resources (UN/INTOSAI, 2015). By holding governments accountable, SAIs play an important role in ensuring that issues of environment sustainability are at the centre of development initiatives (Nombembe, 2007, quoted in WGEA 2007b: 55). Sustainable development worldwide is only possible if the use of public resources is made more transparent and accountable (Moser, 2015) by the work of SAIs.

Due to their position within the national administrative system, generally with a mandate over wide areas of government endeavour and their active involvement in regional and global organizations, SAIs can make significant contributions towards the successful achievement of SDGs (Dutra, 2016). They can take a long-term perspective of the issues (Oviir, 2012) and can better integrate social, economic and environmental issues across different sectors and form non-partisan views – a basic requirement for auditing sustainable development programmes. Due to their ability to understand local circumstances, SAIs are honest brokers of assessments of government policies at the national level. As such, their performance audits are a great tool to support monitoring and evaluation of the SDGs (Lapointe, 2015). UN Resolution A/66/209 of December 2011 recognized 'the important role SAIs play in promoting the efficiency, accountability and transparency of public administration' and called for their strengthening to promote good governance. Subsequently, UN Resolution A/C.2/69/L.25/Rev1 of November 2014 acknowledged the role of SAIs in fostering governmental accountability for the use of resources and their performance in achieving development goals, including internationally agreed development goals. SAIs are at the core of effective, accountable and transparent institutions (Hongbo, 2015). SAIs-related target 16.6 of the SDGs perhaps reflects learning from the implementation of MDGs that had inadequate monitoring and evaluation framework (Lapointe, 2015). These UN resolutions anchor the important role of SAIs in the post-2015 development agenda (Sattler, 2015). Further, the UN Secretary General has expressly stressed the need for strengthening SAIs as the national oversight mechanism in the *Synthesis Report on Post-2015 Agenda* (UN, 2014: paragraphs 92, 145–150).

Limited literature on environmental performance auditing

On one hand, SAIs and their performance auditing are considered critical to achieving environmental sustainability and SDGs; on the other, compared with thousands of papers on environmental evaluation (Prasad, 2016: 7), there has been very little academic work (about a dozen papers) on environment-related performance auditing. Some lead papers are noted herein. Rubenstein (2001) observes that performance auditing is a vital link between stewards of the environment and those to whom they are accountable. He describes the audits undertaken by the Canadian Commissioner of Environment and the role it can play in empowering the public. Rose (2001) explored the practice and possibilities of auditing the performance of the Australian government's environmental commitments. He also commented on the then debate for establishing a national Commissioner for the Environment for this purpose. Van Leeuwen (2004a) describes the results of the first three International Organization of Supreme Audit Institutions (INTOSAI) Working Group on Environmental Auditing (WGEA) surveys on environmental auditing by SAIs. Van Leeuwen (2004b) discusses the procedural aspects of international cooperation in environmental auditing through the WGEA. She notes the need for future research into the contribution of the environmental audit work of SAIs to the improvement of environmental governance and policy performance, and the advantages of international cooperation between SAIs on audits of international environmental agreements. Rika (2009) investigates environmental auditing by the SAI of Fiji and notes that it is strongly motivated by the UN system, including INTOSAI. Martinov-Bennie and Hecimovic (2010) describe the assurance-related challenges involved in auditing the performance of regional public sector natural resource management (NRM) bodies, e.g. catchment management agencies by the Natural Resource Commission (NRC) of the Australian State of New South Wales. This study is not about an SAI in that the NRC is both a judge and advocate of NRM. However, Martinov-Bennie and Hecimovic's suggestion for research into the issues of independence of audit and audit methodology is relevant here. Lima and Magrini (2010) describe the Brazilian Audit Tribunal's role in external auditing of environmental management in Brazil. Yusoff (2013) explores the understanding of the public sector auditors about the environmental audit. Wang et al. (2011) and Liu and Xu (2014) discuss environmental performance auditing in China and suggest some measures for improvement. Rika (2014) examines environmental performance auditing at the SAI of Australia and concludes that environmental performance auditing is essentially used as a tool to manage reputational risk in the public sector.

Other than descriptive individual audit reports and guidelines, there is very limited investigative work available on environmental performance auditing in professional (non-academic) literature. For example: RPC (2010) discusses environmental performance auditing in China and suggests a few ideas for overcoming some related challenges; INTOSAI (2012) describes the current and future challenges of environmental auditing; and Reed and Cing-Mars (2014) discuss ways of increasing the impact of environmental performance audits.

Reasons, purpose and scope of this book

Overall, the few academic studies noted above that have investigated some aspects of environmental performance auditing point to the need for further investigation. Further, most of the work on performance auditing generally is related to developed countries (e.g. Lonsdale et al., 2011; Pollitt et al., 1999). There is no previous work that has investigated environmental performance auditing undertaken by SAIs taking a global perspective. This book endeavours to fill this knowledge gap. The three main objectives of this book are: (1) to understand what has been the trend in environmental performance auditing; (2) to understand how environmental performance auditing is currently practised; and (3) to understand issues and challenges in environmental performance auditing.

This book is focused on environmental performance audits undertaken only by SAIs. It is a strategic volume aimed at practitioners, such as performance audit managers and auditors general, academics, and decision makers in government, donor agencies and other international organizations (e.g. UN bodies such as UNEP) who are interested in broader issues related to environmental performance auditing, such as relevant trends and capacity development. The book is not intended to be a comprehensive text on performance auditing. Not being about technical auditing, it is not aimed at theoretically inclined readers who want to see more use of models and statistical analysis.

Structure of the book

Chapter 1 (this chapter) establishes the need, purpose and scope and provides an outline of the book.

For the benefit of readers who are not necessarily experts in auditing, Chapter 2 starts with the conceptual and institutional framework of performance auditing. As performance auditing continues to be a work in progress, its identity and nature continue to be debated. The contemporary debate over the nature of performance auditing, such as the effectiveness of process or effectiveness of outcome, is briefly noted, followed by a description of how performance auditing is undertaken. Having established this context, the chapter differentiates the concept of environmental auditing in the public sector from that in the private sector. It further clarifies the difference between environmental performance auditing and the nearby concept of the state of environment reporting. The chapter ends by noting the special challenges associated with performance auditing in the environmental domain and argues the case for its recognition as a specialist branch of performance auditing.

Chapter 3 investigates global trends in environmental performance auditing through quantitative analyses of (1) two decades (1992–2012) of global environmental performance audit data; and (2) eight global survey results. The former analysis also considers some socio-economic data (such as per capita gross national income and developmental status of countries) available from the World Bank to investigate whether socio-economic factors influence environmental performance auditing. In addition to discovering trends, the analysis identifies SAIs that have not undertaken environmental performance auditing. The SAIs that have not published any environmental performance audits during the two decades 1992–2012 are considered as likely not to have undertaken any environmental performance audits. The SAIs having experience in conducting environmental performance audits identified here can serve as a source of information on the current practice of environmental performance auditing. They form the target group for a global survey of SAIs that is undertaken in Chapter 4.

Through a global survey of SAIs, Chapter 4 investigates the current practice (i.e. the state of the craft) in environmental performance auditing, such as how they select environmental topics for audit; what methods they use for evidence collection; how they frame audit criteria; the standards and guidelines they use for quality assurance of audits; the impact their audits have created; and challenges they face in undertaking environmental performance. This chapter also investigates the benefits of cooperation among SAIs. In addition to presenting the overall global picture of practice, the chapter also presents the analysis of the results in terms of developed and developing country SAIs to discern any differences due to the difference in their socio-economic status.

Taking a diagnostic approach to learning, Chapter 5 explores the practice of environmental performance auditing in three countries – Australia, Canada and India – through a review of their environmental performance audit reports over a five-year period (2010–2014). The chapter describes in a comparative analytical manner how each SAI has treated the key attributes of performance audits, such as audit objectives, audit criteria, methods for evidence gathering, argumentation, reporting style and audit recommendations. In doing so, the chapter also analyses how each SAI's audit reports ('what is') compare with the requirements of their own relevant standards, manuals and guidelines ('what should be'). The chapter highlights both good practices and areas of improvement.

Chapter 6 brings together the barriers and challenges to environmental performance auditing discovered in investigations presented in Chapters 3, 4 and 5. The barriers and challenges identified relate to matters largely outside the control of SAIs, such as deficiencies in monitoring and reporting, resources and mandate of SAIs. However, sometimes through their own actions SAIs manage to overcome them. The chapter also describes the policy learnings acquired by SAIs through their environmental performance audits.

Chapter 7 concludes the book by bringing together the learning in earlier chapters. It synthesizes the key underlying issues discovered in the investigations presented and discusses their prospects into the future. The chapter also identifies some measures that need to be taken to meet the current and emerging challenges of environmental performance auditing, especially in the context of achieving the sustainable development goals (SDGs).

Note

1 The highest-level of public auditing body (National Auditor General) of a country is its Supreme Audit Institution.

References

Barrett, P. (2001). Evaluation and performance auditing: sharing the common ground. Paper presented at the Australasian Evaluation Society International Conference.

Chertow, M. R. & Esty, D. C. (1997). *Thinking Ecologically: The Next Generation of Environmental Policy*. London: Yale University Press.

Durant, R. F., Fiorino, D. J. & O'Leary, R. (2004). *Environmental Governance Reconsidered: Challenges, Choices, and Opportunities*. Cambridge, MA: MIT Press.

Dutra, P. H. (2016). SDGs audit results framework. *International Journal of Government Auditing*, 43(1), 12–14.

Fiorino, D. J. (2001). Environmental policy as learning: a new view of an old landscape. *Public Administration Review*, 61(3), 322–334.

Holden, E., Linnerud, K. & Banister, D. (2014). Sustainable development: our common future revisited. *Global Environmental Change*, 26, 130–139.

Hongbo, W. (2015). Accountability for sustainable development. Retrieved 26 March 2016, from www.un.org/en/development/desa/news/administration/unintosai-symposium.html.

ICSU. (2017). New report from scientific experts provides a unique guide to translate Sustainable Development Goals into reality. Retrieved 17 May 2017, from www.icsu.org/current/press/new-report-from-scientific-experts-provides-a-unique-guide-to-translate-sustainable-development-goals-into-reality.

INCOSAI. (2010). Johannesburg Accord. Paper presented at the International Congress of Supreme Audit Institutions (NCOSAI) XX, Johannesburg, South Africa.

INTOSAI. (2012). Environmental auditing: current and future challenges. *International Journal of Government Auditing*, 39(3), 21–22.

Keene, M. & Pullin, A. S. (2011). Realizing an effectiveness revolution in environmental management. *Journal of Environmental Management*, 92(9), 2130–2135.

Lapointe, C. (2015). What lessons learned and advice SAIs can share from reviewing the implementation of the MDGs for the SDGs. Paper presented at the 23rd UN/INTOSAI Symposium: 'UN Post-2015 Development Agenda: The Role of SAIs and Means of Implementation for Sustainable Development'.

Lima, L. H. & Magrini, A. (2010). The Brazilian Audit Tribunal's role in improving the federal environmental licensing process. *Environmental Impact Assessment Review*, 30(2), 108–115.

Liu, Y. & Xu, Q. (2014) Study on government environmental performance audit. *Advanced Materials Research*, 962–965, 2072–2075.

Lonsdale, J., Ling, T. & Wilkins, P. (2011). *Performance Auditing: Contributing to Accountability in Democratic Government*. Cheltenham: Edward Elgar.

Martinov-Bennie, N. & Hecimovic, A. (2010). Assurance of Australian natural resource management. *Public Management Review*, 12(4), 549–565.

Moser, J. (2015). The important role of SAIs in the UN post-2015 development agenda. *International Journal of Government Auditing*, 42(1), 1–3.

Oviir, M. (2012). Environmental auditing in INTOSAI: 20 years later. *International Journal of Government Auditing*, 39(3), 1–5).

Pollitt, C. & Summa, H. (1996). Performance audit and evaluation: similar tools, different relationships? *New Directions for Evaluation*, 71, 29–50.

Pollitt, C., Girre, X., Lonsdale, J., Mul, R., Summa, H. & Waerness, M. (1999). *Performance or Compliance? Performance Audit and Public Management in Five Countries*. Oxford: Oxford University Press.

Prasad, A. (2016). Environmental Performance Auditing by Supreme Audit Institutions: Progress, Practice and Prospects. PhD thesis, The Australian National University, Canberra. Retrieved 15 April 2017 from http://hdl.handle.net/1885/112881

Reed, J. & Cinq-Mars, J. (2014). How to increase the impact of environmental performance audits. *International Journal of Government Auditing*, 41(2), 17–23.
Rika, N. (2009). What motivates environmental auditing? A public sector perspective. *Pacific Accounting Review*, 21(3), 304–318.
Rika, N. (2014). Reputational risk and environmental performance auditing in the public sector: framing and overflows in the audit process. Thesis, Australian National University, Canberra.
Rose, G. (2001). Environmental performance auditing of government: The role for an Australian Commissioner for the Environment. *Environmental and Planning Law Journal*, 18(3), 293–318.
RPC. (2010). Performance audit of the Liaoning environmental research. Retrieved 27 January 2017, from http://webcache.googleusercontent.com/search?q=cache:http://eng.hi138.com/accounting-and-auditing-papers/audit-papers/201003/219631_performance-audit-of-the-liaoning-environmental-research.asp&gws_rd=cr&ei=06uWWMmRKsem8AX6sa3QDQ#.WJar1Pl97IU
Rubenstein, D.B. (2001). Audit as an agent of constructive consequence and social change. *Corporate Environmental Strategy*, 8(3), 234–241.
Sattler, R. (2015). UN Resolution A 69/228. *International Journal of Government Auditing*, 42(2), 39–41.
Taalas, P (2017). World Meterological Organisation (WMO) presentation to the 23rd annual 'Conference of the Parties' (COP).
Topfer, K. (2004). Environmental auditing and sustainable development: SAIs matter. *International Journal of Government Auditing*, 32(2), 1–4.
UN. (2014). *A/69/700-4 December 2014: The Road to Dignity by 2030: Ending Poverty, Transforming All Lives and Protecting the Planet: Synthesis Report of the Secretary-General on the post-2015 Sustainable Development Agenda*. New York: United Nations.
UN-DSD. (2017). Sustainable Development Knowledge Platform. Retrieved 17 October 2017, from https://sustainabledevelopment.un.org/about.
UNDP. (2016). A new sustainable development agenda. Retrieved 22 March 2016, from www.undp.org/content/undp/en/home/sdgoverview.
UNEP. (2010). Auditing the Implementation of Multilateral Environmental Agreements (MEAs): A Primer for Auditors. Nairobi: UNEP.
UNEP. (2012). Global Environment Outlook: Summary for Policy Makers GEO5. Nairobi: UNEP.
UN/INTOSAI. (2015). Report on the 23rd UN/INTOSAI Symposium, 'UN Post-2015 Development Agenda: The Role of SAIs and Means of Implementation for Sustainable Development', Vienna, 2–4 March.
UN-WSSD. (2002). *Plan of Implementation of the World Summit on Sustainable Development*. New York: United Nations.
Van Leeuwen, S. (2004a). Developments in environmental auditing by supreme audit institutions. *Environmental Management*, 33(2), 163–172.
Van Leeuwen, S. (2004b). Auditing international environmental agreements: the role of supreme audit institutions. *Environmentalist*, 24(2), 93–99.
Wang, J., Zhang, B. & Chen, T. (2011). The case study of China's environmental audit: taking the Taihu Lake as an example. *Energy Procedia*, 5, 2108–2113.
WCED (1987). *Our Common Future*. New York: World Commission on Environment and Development, United Nations
WGEA. (2007a). *Fifth Survey on Environmental Auditing: INTOSAI Working Group on Environmental Auditing*. Vienna: WGEA.

WGEA. (2007b). *Evolution and Trends in Environmental Auditing*. Stockholm: INTOSAI Working Group on Environmental Auditing.

WGEA. (2012). *Improving National Performance: Environmental Auditing Supports Better Governance and Management*: Vienna: WGEA

Yusoff, H.N. (2013). Understanding environmental audit in the public sector: Malaysian perspective. *Jurnal Teknologi*, 62(1), 25–30.

2 Environmental performance auditing

This chapter provides an overview of key concepts related to auditing, such as why an audit is undertaken, the types of audits and institutional mechanisms for auditing. Though auditing is considered the 'third oldest' profession after 'trade' and 'accounting' (Rubenstein, 2001), it would be overly optimistic to assume that all readers possess equal or sufficient background understanding as the necessary foundation for the remainder of the book.

Audit, its origin and rationale

Audit is a judgement about 'what is' compared with 'what should be', using the prevalent 'moral, social, political, economic and legal norms' of the relationship between the 'stewards of the human enterprise' and to whom they are accountable, where a 'steward' is one who manages another's property (Rubenstein, 2001). A relationship of accountability is the primary condition for audit, where a duty of acceptable conduct is owed by one party (steward) to the other party or parties – the principal (Flint, 1988: 23). Furubo (2011) considers that while it is possible for a principal to scrutinize the steward, it is easier to have a third party – the auditor – to conduct this scrutiny (Furubo, 2011). The independence of the third party is a prerequisite for audit (Flint, 1988: 23).

Audit is 'one of the oldest and most venerable state functions' (Pollitt and Summa, 1999) and is as old as civilization itself (CAG, 2010: 5; Kells and Hodge, 2009). Large public works such as pyramids were undertaken by central governments with public money that required auditing (Rubenstein, 2001). Public auditing appeared in 'an embryonic form in the Western Zhou Dynasty of China some 3000 years ago' (Adams, 1986: 189). Public auditors existed in ancient India (CAG, 2010: 5), in Persia (Farazmand, 1998; Hodge, 2009), Rome (Burrowes and Persson, 2000: 85) and ancient Greece (Normanton, 1966). Ancient Egypt and Babylon, too, had embryonic public auditing (Burrowes and Persson, 2000: 85). By the twelfth century, England had a highly centralized administrative kingship that was ruled through centralized auditing and semi-annual account-giving based upon the Domesday Books developed in the eleventh century as the basis for taxation and royal governance (Bovens, 2006: 6), and this became more formal 200 years later. The UK National Audit Office

(NAO) cites its first manifestation in 1314; the French Cour des Comptes traces its origins back to 1318; and the Dutch Algemene Rekenkamer identifies its ancestors back to 1386 (Pollitt and Summa, 1999). Burrowes and Persson (2000: 85) and Jurado-Sánchez (2002) note that Isabella, Queen of Castile, sent an auditor with Columbus to ensure he accounted for the profits from his voyages to the Indies.

As 'disease' is the reason for the 'profession of medicine', 'distrust' is the reason for audit (Rubenstein, 2001). 'The political and administrative history of all ages' has shown 'without the shadow of doubt' that in all forms of government 'sooner or later, there is an abuse of power, when external punitive controls are lacking' (Finer, 1965: 179). While the 'bad guy' perception of public administration may be the main reason for audit, the 'good guy' image also requires audit (Furubo, 2011). The information produced serves different purposes in the two cases. While the 'bad guy' audit provides information to curb the abuse of power, the 'good guy' audit produces information that enables improvement (Furubo, 2011).

Types of audit

Audits are generally of three types: (1) financial; (2) compliance (with rules and laws); and (3) performance. The first two together are also known as a regularity audit, whose main purpose is attestation (INTOSAI, 2010). Performance audit, on the other hand, is 'an independent examination of the efficiency and effectiveness of government undertakings, programs or organisations with due regard to economy, and the aim of leading to improvement' (INTOSAI, 2004: 11). While a financial audit is generally an annual cycle of 'checking of the books', a performance audit is an individually tailored project (Summa, 1999) undertaken on a non-recurring basis (INTOSAI, 2004: 12). A form of compliance audit is the *a-priori* audit that focuses on the legality of a transaction. Expenditure processing in some countries requires an *a-priori* auditor signing off each document for legitimacy, legality and completeness. In recent times, *a-priori* auditing has become synonymous with real-time auditing that examines transactions offline in real time for their legitimacy, legality and completeness (Dye, 2007).

Performance auditing is almost unique to the public sector (Pollitt, 1999; Summa, 1999a) and does not have its roots common to the private sector (INTOSAI, 2004:12). The differences between the two forms of audit, however, should not be over-emphasized. They both exist for the reason of accountability. In government or public auditing, even financial auditing includes audit areas, other than just audit of accounts; and performance auditing includes examination of economy (Suzuki, 2004). Suzuki (2004) observes that comprehensive public accountability requires both financial accountability and performance accountability, noting a paradigm shift from mere accountability 'for the use of public money' (the domain of traditional financial audit) to 'public accountability' for performance that includes auditing 'economy, efficiency and effectiveness'. Consistent with this reasoning, INTOSAI (2004: 12) cautions against 'undermining collaboration between the two types of auditing'.

Performance auditing

Compared to traditional auditing, that is as old as the history of human civilization (Kells and Hodge, 2009), performance auditing is a recent activity originating in the mid to late twentieth century. Four periods are cited as being the beginning of modern performance auditing in the literature: the post-Second World War era (Lonsdale, 2000), the 1950s (Shand and Anand, 1996: 58), the 1960s (Adams, 1986: 189) and the 1970s (Pollitt and Summa, 1999). Kells and Hodge (2009), who trace the chronology of modern performance auditing, note that while its temporal origin is unclear, Sweden, Japan, Germany, the USA and Canada are all valid spatial origins of modern performance auditing. Modern performance auditing has subsequently spread to other countries in the British Commonwealth (Lapsley and Pong, 2000) and Eastern Europe (Jones, 2008), probably from these origins. Barrett (Former Auditor General of Australia, personal communication) considers that the UK has been one of the pioneers of performance auditing. He further observes that performance auditing started in Australia as efficiency audits in the late 1970s. Pollitt and Summa (1999) note that performance auditing is connected to the new public management (NPM) that allowed flexibility in terms of inputs and processes ('letting the managers manage') in return for a stronger focus on monitoring and evaluating performance (outputs and outcomes).

There are two main purposes of performance auditing: accountability and learning for improvement (Barzelay, 1996; Lonsdale, 2000; Pollitt and Summa, 1997). Supreme Audit Institutions (SAIs), in conducting performance audits, are on a double mission. They provide independent assurance about the performance of the public sector (Barrett, 2012) and make recommendations for improving the performance of audited organizations (Kells, 2011). English et al. (2010) call accountability a 'watch dog' role and learning for improvement a 'sheep dog' role, imploring that performance audits 'involve going beyond a "watchdog" to a "sheepdog" role', particularly, but not exclusively, in relation to effectiveness. However, there is a tension between the 'watchdog' function (drawing attention to failure) and the 'sheep dog' function (guiding agencies and departments towards better practice), as 'watchdogs do not make good sheepdogs' (Ling, 2003: 444). The inherent tension and/or conflict in the dual role has been noted by several others (e.g. Barrett, 2012; Funkhouser, 2011; Loocke and Put, 2011).

Performance auditing is a work in progress

The International Congress of Supreme Audit Institutions (INCOSAI), as early as 1986, defined performance audit as an 'audit which is concerned with evaluation of economy, efficiency and effectiveness of public sector management' (INCOSAI, 1986). Notwithstanding the existence of this definition and its subsequent adoption in a standard by INTOSAI (2004), the nature of performance auditing continues to be debated in the literature. For example, Barzelay (1996: 19) calls performance auditing a misnomer, observing that it is an evaluating activity of type, whose name happens to include the word 'auditing'. Kells and Hodge (2009) reject the construct of three Es (economy, efficiency and effectiveness) as the core of performance auditing and instead offer a five-element definition that incorporates independence, authorization, discovery, synthesis and publication. Furubo (2011) argues that performance auditing is a form of 'conceptual stretching' (Sartori, 1970: 1033), whereby audit offices extended their 'traditional territory of financial audit', and legitimized it by calling it 'auditing'. Noting ambiguity in the INTOSAI definition, Furubo (2011) proposes a new definition starting from first principles, as follows:

> Performance auditing is an *evaluative activity which produces assessments* regarding *performance* or information about performance of such a *reliable* degree and with such a *freedom from investigatory and reporting constraints* that they can be used in the realm of *accountability*. (Emphasis added)

The two new definitions almost a quarter-century after the one proposed by an authoritative body show that the nature and identity of performance auditing remain a work in progress. Some issues that continue to be debated in relation to performance auditing include:

(1) The idea of effectiveness: (a) is it related to policy (substantive effectiveness); or only to the process of implementation (administrative effectiveness)? (b) Alternatively, is outcome being assessed or is only the system/process to achieve outcome being assessed? Most performance audits take the accountability (systemic/administrative) approach and consequently use notionally so-called 'good management' criteria and test if those have been adhered to. Such an approach is low-risk and is conceptually not different from financial auditing (Pollitt, 1999: 205). It does not address the substantive effectiveness that requires venturing into a political territory not necessarily preferred by SAIs. Noting significant developments since Pollitt made that observation, Barrett (Former Auditor General of Australia, personal communication) however, notes that many performance audits go beyond a good management approach. Assessing whether policy objectives are being met economically, efficiently and effectively does not necessarily always require an entry into the political domain (Barrett, personal communication).
(2) Efficiency or effectiveness: a highly efficient system can be ineffective (fail to achieve the objective) and an inefficient system can still be reasonably effective.
(3) Accountability: who is ultimately accountable – the government (minister) to the parliament and people, or the administration to the government?
(4) The accountability mission of performance auditing does not sit well with the learning mission. While the former (traditional assurance mode of audit) is based on social distance between the auditor and auditee, the latter is based upon social proximity between the two (Morin 2003; Saint-Martin, 2004).

> Thus, the improvement mission of performance auditing is not consistent with the institutional position of SAIs (Barzelay, 1997; Morin, 2003; Saint-Martin, 2004). Also, while the accountability approach does not require extensive expert knowledge of the matter, the learning approach does require such knowledge (Put, 2011). Given that it is almost impossible for SAIs to have expert knowledge of all areas of government business, it raises the question of how their performance audits can contribute to improvements in areas where they do not have expertise. The issue of expertise becomes very important in specialist areas such as the environment. While the two objectives can and do co-exist comfortably in most cases, in the case of conflict, accountability will prevail. It is to be noted that some of the challenges that performance auditing faces are also due to its comparatively recent history. Unlike the thousands of years old history of financial accountability, performance accountability is less than 50 years old. So, performance auditing is still evolving and thus it is not unexpected to have ongoing debate on its nature.

Related to this debate is the inability of SAIs, particularly in the Westminster system, to comment on the merits of government policy. The continuing debate in the performance audit literature over the policy versus implementation audit is contentious. There are contrasting views on the matter even among practitioners. For example, Barrett (2015) – a former Auditor General of Australia – citing evidence in performance audit reports, observes that deficiency in programme performance is frequently more about policy than implementation. On the other hand, Emmett (1996) – who later became the first Commissioner of Environment and Sustainable Development (CESD) within the Canadian Office of Auditor General (OAG) – did not see any downside to the necessity for the CESD being a part of the OAG to keep away from policy debate, observing, 'the biggest problem on the environmental side at the moment is the gap between policy and execution. What we need are better systems to execute policies that are formed by parliament and by ministers.'

Supreme Audit Institutions

An SAI is the highest public audit body of a country responsible for auditing: (a) the regularity of government accounts (expenditure and receipts); and (b) performance of its policies and programmes. Due to their diverse cultural and political history, SAIs significantly differ among themselves in terms of their structure, mandate and types of audit they conduct. However, there are three common models of SAIs (WGEA, 2007a: 10):

- Westminster or Anglo-Saxon model, also called 'Audit Office';
- judicial or Napoleonic model, also called 'Court of Audit' or 'Court of Accounts'; and
- collegiate model, also called 'Board of Audit'.

The 'Audit Offices' are intrinsically related to the legislature (e.g. parliament) through public account committees (PACs) or similar bodies. In many countries, they are independent from the executive arm of the government and headed by a single senior official called the Auditor General or Comptroller General. The NAO of the UK, the Australian National Audit Office (ANAO), the US Government Accountability Office (GAO), the offices of the Comptroller and Audit General (CAG) of India and New Zealand are examples of this model. Strategic and open communication to parliament and the public is critically important in this model (WGEA, 2007a: 10).

The 'Courts of Audit' are an integral part of the judicial system. The top members are judges, one of whom presides over the 'Court'. Staff of the Courts are from legal rather than accounting backgrounds. Courts are independent and traditionally have dealt with financial and compliance matters. They hold government officials accountable for public monies and can fine them. Compared with the Audit Offices, they have a lesser relationship with the legislature. However, their reports can highlight matters that are of interest to the legislature. The French Cour des Comptes is an example of the judicial model of SAIs (WGEA, 2007a: 10).

In the 'collegiate or Board' model, the SAI is part of the legislature's system of accountability. The 'Boards of Audit' are structured similar to 'Courts', however, without any judicial power. The 'Boards' are headed by one of its members. Each member has an audit portfolio and possesses significant autonomy (WGEA, 2007a: 10). The SAI of Germany is an example of the 'collegiate' model.

An SAI can be a combination of the three basic types and can have judicial functions as well as be related to the legislature at the same time to a varying degree. For example, though SAIs of many developing countries originated under a British/French colonial model ('Audit Office' or 'Court'), they have subsequently been modified to incorporate features of other models preferred by donor agencies (WGEA, 2007a: 10).

Standards and guidelines for performance audits

The quality of performance audits is critical to the reputation and credibility of SAIs (Wilkins and Boyle, 2011). 'Professional standards are most evident in the area of performance audits and are strongly supported by audit offices' as a means of ensuring their credibility (Mayne and Schwartz, 2005). Acknowledging the diversity in performance audit practices across different countries, INTOSAI (2004) has set the international performance auditing standards (ISSAI 3000-3100) as non-mandatory guidelines. These guidelines are a set of principles outlining a shared understanding of high-quality work. The emphasis here is on judgement and interpretation rather than on a 'one size fits all' approach. INTOSAI (2004: 29) cautions against streamlining performance auditing, noting that:

> Advanced performance auditing is complex investigatory work that requires flexibility, imagination and high levels of analytical skills. Streamlined

> procedures, methods and standards may, in fact, hamper the functioning and the progress of performance auditing. Consequently, standards—as well as quality assurance systems—that are too detailed should be avoided. Progress and practices must be built on learning from experience.

INTOSAI (2004:13) clearly sets performance auditing apart from financial auditing by observing that, 'while financial auditing tends to apply relatively fixed standards, performance auditing is more flexible in its choice of subjects, audit objects, methods, and opinions'. Unlike traditional financial auditing, performance auditing 'is not a check-list based auditing' (INTOSAI, 2004: 13). Rather than calling for uniform global standards for performance auditing, INTOSAI (2004) advocates that each SAI should have its own policy on quality that has regard to INTOSAI standards and other professional standards relevant to their work (INTOSAI-ISSAI, 2004: 1). Accordingly, several countries have their own standards or mandatory guidelines for performance auditing. Wilkins and Boyle (2011) have compared the standards of the UK's NAO, USA's GAO and Australia's ANAO with INTOSAI standards. According to them, two distinct approaches to standards for performance auditing have emerged. One is harder, prescriptive and originates from financial auditing standards and is exemplified by the ANAO standard, ASAE 3500 (AASB, 2008). The other is softer, based upon principles and quality thresholds encompassing research and methodological approaches of diverse disciplines, and is exemplified by NAO. The latter is more in line with the INTOSAI approach.

Standards are helpful in many ways, such as in ensuring consistency across different audits, enabling clarity in internal and external communications and assuring the audience of the quality of the audit report. However, consistency may come at the cost of innovation and may limit adapting performance audits to specific contexts, especially when they are mandatory (Wilkins and Boyle, 2011). While desirable, codifying everything is not necessarily the best way forward; SAIs should not be overly concerned about the codification; they should be more concerned about being authoritative and independent judges of performance, rather than being an authoritative source of evidence of performance (Lonsdale et al., 2011a: 316–317).

Performance audit process

The performance auditing cycle involves three key stages: (A) planning (strategic planning and preparatory work); (B) execution/conduct of audit; and (C) follow-up activities. In addition to the INTOSAI (2004) guidelines, usually each SAI would have its own guidelines for performance auditing that cover these matters in detail (see, for example, the Australian SAI's Guidelines for the Conduct of Performance Audits (ANAO, 2015b)). The three phases of performance audit, A (Pre-audit), B (Audit) and C (Post-Audit) as followed by the Australian SAI (ANAO, 2015b) are shown schematically in Figure 2.1.

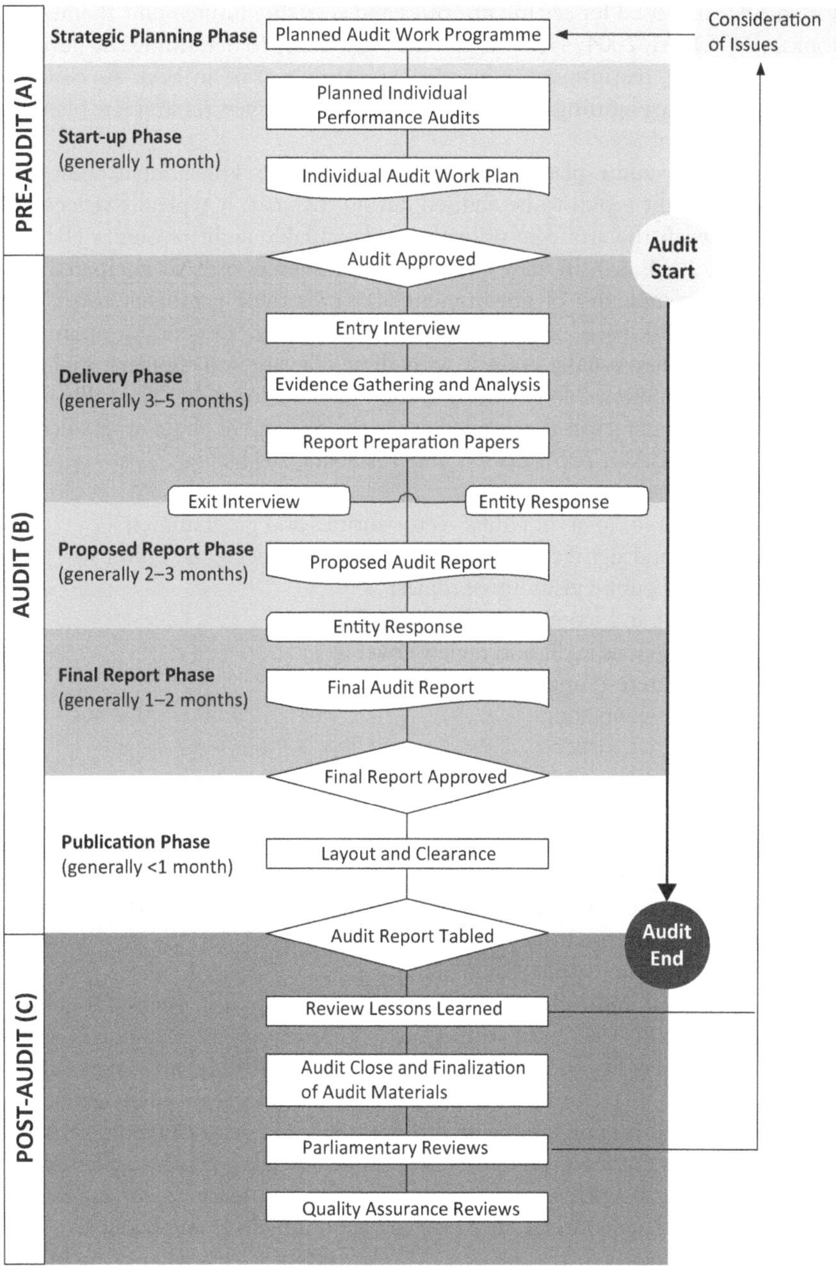

Figure 2.1 Performance audit phases.

Source: adapted with permission from ANAO, 2015b.

A1: Strategic planning. This is the process for determining long-term goals for an SAI. It is used for setting priorities and selecting future audit themes and topics (INTOSAI, 2004: 47). It is also used internally to determine the development needs (e.g. recruitment, education and training) of an SAI. As common with any strategic planning document, an SAI would review its strategic planning at regular intervals.

A2: Annual audit plan and selection of topics. The annual audit plan contains the audit topics to be audited during the year. It typically reflects the balance between the strategic priorities and available audit resources (Barrett, 2012; CAG, 2014: 21). In view of the limited resources of SAIs compared with the size and complexity of government activities their mandates cover, they usually take a risk-based approach in selecting topics. Depending upon their legal position, they usually consult with their relevant stakeholders, including auditees, and sometimes do pay heed to their requests for audit. The following is an indicative list of factors that contribute to the judgement about topic selection (ANAO, 2014; CAG, 2014: 22; Put and Turksema, 2011):

- risks in different areas of public sector entities and programmes;
- materiality and significance, including financial, social and political;
- salience and public visibility of topics;
- likely impact and scope for improvement;
- extent of previous audit and review coverage;
- legislature interest; and
- need for follow-up audit.

While acknowledging that SAIs do provide information on their approach to topic selection, and hence are transparent, Put and Turksema (2011) note the need for more research into topic selection to gain insight into individual organizational and external factors influencing the decision-making process. It is interesting to note that international organizations, such as INTOSAI, sometimes determine the sectoral audit topics (e.g. WGEA for the environment) through their planning cycle (Rika, 2009).

A3: Individual audit plan. The final step of the planning phase is the development of an individual audit work plan that defines the scope and objectives and outlines the audit criteria; methods to be used; schedule; and budget of the audit (ANAO, 2014). During this step, the audit team develops an understanding of the entity and the programme or activity subject to audit, including through preliminary consultation with entity/programme officials and other stakeholders, such as relevant industry groups. This enables a detailed plan to be prepared including audit scope, criteria, methods and audit schedules and budget.

The audit objective(s) is an essential element of a performance audit that defines the intention or purpose of the audit, and must be expressed in a way that allows drawing conclusion against them (ANAO, 2015a: 72). They are the reasons for conducting the audit (CAG, 2014: 27) and usually include the questions the audit will answer about the performance of an activity, such as results achieved, economy and efficiency (OAG, 2004: 49). As future audit effort will be directed towards answering the questions raised in the audit objectives, they must be defined as clearly as possible to avoid any unnecessary and costly audit work (OAG, 2004: 49). To make them clearer, audit objectives can be divided into sub-objectives. However, sub-objectives should be complementary, not overlapping, and collectively be exhaustive in addressing the overall objective (CAG, 2014: 10). The audit objectives largely determine the audit approach and audit criteria (ANAO, 2015a: 73; CAG, 2014: 10). It is quite possible that audit objectives might change during the audit. However, quality assurance processes of SAIs would normally require that such changes are authorized before the audit report is finalized (see, for example, ANAO, 2015a: 100; OAG, 2004: 49).

There are three approaches available in performance auditing that can be taken separately or in combination (CAG, 2014: 10; INTOSAI-ISSAI, 2004: 3).

- **System-oriented approach:** examines the proper functioning of management or control systems, e.g. the financial management system. The focus here is on the adequacy of systems (policies and procedures) to promote, monitor and evaluate performance (OAG, 2004: 55) for achieving economy, efficiency and effectiveness (Daujotait and Mačerinskien, 2008).
- **Result-oriented approach:** assesses whether programme objectives have been achieved as intended. The audit focuses on inputs, outputs, results and impacts (OAG, 2004: 55).
- **Problem-oriented approach:** verifies and analyses the causes of a particular problem(s).

Of the three approaches listed, the first two, or a combination thereof, are more commonly used (Daujotait and Mačerinskien, 2008; OAG, 2004: 55).

Audit criteria/norms are either derived from official sources (e.g. entity's enabling legislation, entity's own policy or definition of performance); or SAIs frame their own definition of performance, such as using professional literature, expert advice and benchmarking (CAG, 2014: 29–30; Put, 2011). Put (2011) observes that the official norms are more defensible and cheaper to establish; they serve the accountability paradigm by enabling a check of whether entities are conforming to their own standards. On the other hand, the second (pluralist) category of norms requires more effort to develop and serve the improvement paradigm better (Put, 2011). Official norms may be prone to gaming and even be questionable if policy objectives are unrealistic, being either too easy or too ambitious (Put, 2011).

Supreme Audit Institutions use various methods (Table 2.1) for evidence collection. However, there is no universally acceptable nomenclature and listing of methods. For example, each of the two well-cited texts on performance audit (Pollitt et al., 1999: 129 – 16 methods; and Lonsdale et al., 2011b: 100 – 23 methods) and INTOSAI publications (INTOSAI, 2004: 96–99 – 7 methods; and

Table 2.1 Methods used for evidence collection in performance audits

Basic methods	*Specialized methods*
Document examination	System/process review (including database)
Interview of officials	Literature survey
Questionnaire/survey	Case study
Stakeholders consultation/survey	Benchmarking
Site visit	Focus group
Sample examination	Economical/statistical analysis
Expert opinion	Scientific modelling (e.g. hydrological, ecological)

WGEA, 2013: 51 – 12 methods) variously list and describe the methods. This may create interpretational difficulties, especially for less commonly used methods, as will be seen in Chapter 5. It is highly desirable to have a standard definition of various methods so that a common understanding of various methods develops and interpretational differences are minimized. Leadership by the INTOSAI on the matter is warranted. To help the standardization process, a description of various methods is given in Appendix A.

Factors that affect the choice of methods include constraints (of time, cost and evidence expectations) and influences at team, project, organizational and environmental levels (Lonsdale, 2011). The appropriate use of methods to generate strong audit evidence is necessary, because audit conclusions are like legal judgments that should be able to withstand legal challenge (Scharaschkin, 2011). Legal standard of evidence is also stressed by Bourn (2007). However, INTOSAI (2004: 60) notes that unlike 'conclusive' evidence required for financial audits, 'persuasive' evidence is sufficient for performance audits.

B: Execution/conduct of audit. While details may vary between SAIs, broadly the following steps are involved.

- **Entry meeting.** Prior to the start of the audit, a meeting is held with officials of the audited body to introduce the audit (background, objectives, scope and schedule of the audit), to advise of the information requirements, and to resolve any issues relating to the audit.
- **Evidence gathering and analysis.** In this phase, evidence is gathered through various methods including document examination and interview of officials (Table 2.1; see Appendix A for detail).
- **Engagement with entity on preliminary conclusion.** Discussion/issue paper(s) containing preliminary conclusions and potential audit recommendations is prepared and provided to the audited entity for feedback, including on any substantive and factual matters.
- **Exit interview.** An exit meeting is conducted to discuss with the entity audit findings, conclusions and potential audit recommendations that have been developed following the feedback.

- **Reporting.** Based on the feedback on the issues paper(s) and any further information provided at the exit interview, a draft report is prepared and sent to the entity for formal comments. The entity's comments are usually included in the final report. This step is quite significant and contentious in that it is effectively a clearance process, in which the entity, if not comfortable with findings, may dispute and obfuscate them, and obstruct and delay the publication of the audit report (Kelly, 1997; Wighton, 1998). The clearance process thus influences what actually goes into the public domain through the final report (Pollitt, 1999). The final report is then submitted either to the parliament or to the body authorizing the audit. The report is usually published.

C: Follow-up. The follow-up facilitates effective implementation of audit recommendations. In parliamentary systems, it typically involves review of audit reports by parliamentary committee(s) and subsequent hearing in some cases. SAIs may also conduct follow-up audits to assess an entity's progress in implementing the recommendations of earlier audits.

Role of civil society organizations in performance auditing

The public audit is now also viewed as a means of community empowerment and agent of social change (see, for example, Rubenstein, 2001; Stern, 2005). When democratic governments all over the world are now endeavouring to build citizen-centric models of public service, there is a case to engage citizens in the accountability mechanism of public service. As end users of government services, citizens are a rich source of knowledge and information about government performance. The twenty-first UN/INTOSAI (2011) Symposium on *Effective Practices of Cooperation between Supreme Audit Institutions and Citizens to Enhance Public Accountability* regarded citizens as 'natural partners' of SAIs and stressed the importance of effective cooperation between SAIs and citizens to protect and promote transparency, accountability and good governance. The twenty-second UN/INTOSAI (2013) Symposium on *Audit and Advisory by SAIs: Risks and Opportunities, as well as Possibilities for Engaging Citizens* recalls UN Resolution A/66/209 that notes that citizens and civil society are as important as addressees of audit reports and recommendations as competent political bodies, and can contribute to effective control through public debate. The symposium emphasized the importance of SAIs' communication of their findings and recommendations in promoting public awareness.

Civil society organizations (CSOs), as representatives of citizens and as consumers and users of public services, are in a strong position to mobilize citizens on public accountability as they have networks and expertise to detect malpractice and report them to SAIs. Bhandari (2014) cites several examples of 'best practice models' of CSO involvement in public audit. While advocating collaboration between SAIs and CSOs, Bhandari (2014) cautions against compromising SAIs' independence in the process. However, with more multilateral and complex programme delivery mechanisms (such as in the environment and sustainable development sector) that include several governments and even the private sector (e.g. public–private partnerships) in a 'steering' rather than 'rowing' governance arrangement, it is logical that audits too will require partnerships.

Impact of performance audits

The impacts of performance audits can be of several types (Loocke and Put, 2011):

- instrumental (work leads to knowledge, and knowledge to policy);
- conceptual (work gradually permeates policy through different means, e.g. insight changes slowly, theories are adopted over time);
- interactive (work results in dialogue between different groups participating in the decision-making process);
- political legitimization (work is used in political debate, such as by an opposition in parliament to establish that a policy is not effective); and
- tactical (work is used to influence a decision, e.g. a decision can be put off pending further investigation).

Performance audits can and do have an impact, though there is limited supporting empirical evidence (Loocke and Put, 2011). Most of the evidence of impact has come from SAIs themselves (Lonsdale, 1999; Morin 2008) who increasingly assess their own performance through indicators such as:

- implementation of audit recommendations;
- audited bodies' views on the value of the SAI's work;
- number of the SAI's reports discussed in parliament;
- parliament's views on the value of the SAI's work;
- frequency of the SAI's coverage in the media; and
- financial impact of the SAI's performance audit.

For example, the USA's GAO estimated that financial benefits of its 2010 audit were US$ 49.9 billion (GAO, 2011a: 2; 2011b: 6). Likewise, the UK's NAO in its 2011 *Annual Report* noted that 'our work in the year led to audited financial impacts of more than £1 billion, improved services to citizens, and increased transparency and accountability' (NAO, 2011: 1).

Notwithstanding the positive claims of SAIs about the impact of performance audits, the related views among academics are mixed (see, for example, Blume and Voigt, 2007; Morin, 2001; 2008; Sutherland, 2003). Some consider the impact on the public sector as 'benign' at best and 'malevolent' at worst (Funkhouser, 2008). Behn (2001) has been scathing, noting that these 'institutions of accountability' are 'nit-picking', as they often pounce on 'small errors' and ultimately undermine public trust that enables government to function well (Behn, 2001: 202–203). Kells' (2011) seven critiques of performance auditing are on similar lines. However, performance audits are considered particularly important for long-term issues such as the environment. 'SAIs are actually the only actors in the public sector who have adequate independence to be able to look farther into the future, even beyond the lifetime of a ruling government' (Oviir, 2012).

Environmental auditing

The term *environmental auditing* originated in the private sector during the 1970s (Rose, 2001) to 1980s (Power, 1994) because of the so-called 'audit explosion' (Power, 1994). Companies started undertaking environmental audits for several reasons, including the requirement of compliance with government environmental regulations to avoid associated penalties, the need for managing civil liability risks, the opportunities for efficiency gains offered by an improved internal management system and the need for a better public image as corporate environmental performance came under increasing public scrutiny (Rose, 2001). 'Environmental auditing' is a convenient label used to denote various types of activities such as management audits, product certification and governmental control measures that have little resemblance to external audit (WGEA, 2012a). As the term 'environmental auditing' is associated with various forms of activities and programmes (Hillary, 1998), different definitions abound in the literature. Because they relate mostly to the private sector, not directly relevant to this book, only some are noted here.

The International Chamber of Commerce (ICC, 1998) provides the most accepted definition of environmental auditing as

> a management tool comprising a systematic, documented, periodic and objective evaluation of how well environmental organization, management and equipment are performing with the aim of helping to safeguard the environment by: (i) facilitating management control of environmental practices; and (ii) assessing compliance with company policies, which would include meeting regulatory requirements.

The ICC definition of environmental audit that is widely accepted by the industry is aimed at the private sector, and is not appropriate to public sector auditing (Rose, 2001).

The International Organisation for Standardisation (ISO) defines environmental auditing as

> a systematic, documented verification process of objectively obtaining and evaluating audit evidence to determine whether specified environmental activities, events, conditions, management systems, or information about these matters, conform with audit criteria, and communicating the results of this process to the client.

Rose (2001) considers that the ISO definition suggests different activities in different circumstances. For example, a one-off project assessment of sediment dredging in port development, or ongoing review of organizational performance, such as internal management of energy efficiency. Accordingly, the term environmental audit is used to denote a wider range of audit procedures, including environmental management system (EMS) audits, compliance audits, site (e.g. contamination) audits, registration/certification audit and industry audit (e.g. mining, timber sector performance) (Rose, 2001).

Environmental auditing in the private sector is essentially an internal audit, or internal control mechanism, that assures the management and investors that the organization operation complies with environmental laws and regulations (Quevedo, 1995; Yusoff, 2013). Legal compliance and exercise of due diligence are the focus of environmental auditing in the private sector. Further, it is used by the management to communicate to clients and stakeholders about the organization's compliance with environmental laws and regulations.

Environmental auditing in the public sector

In contrast to the private sector, environmental auditing in the public sector is considered in terms of the broader framework of accountability to ministers, parliament and ultimately the public (Rose, 2001). Environmental auditing in the public sector undertaken by SAIs solely refers to 'independent external audit of environmental issues' (WGEA, 2012a). It is no different from normal auditing undertaken by SAIs in other fields and may include any combination of three types of audits – financial, compliance and performance (WGEA, 2001: 6). An environmental audit can focus its attention on the disclosure of environmental assets and liabilities, compliance with national and international laws and norms, the implementation of environmental policies and programmes, and to measures taken by the audited body to promote economy, efficiency and effectiveness (Van Leeuwen, 2004; WGEA, 2001: 6). In regards to performance audits, the three Es of economy, effectiveness and efficiency can be considered. However, the inclusion of the fourth E, environment, depends on the SAI's mandate and its government's environmental policy. Sustainable development can be part of the definition of environmental auditing only if it is a part of the government policy and/or programme to be audited (Van Leeuwen, 2004), which is desirable but not necessary for conducting environmental audit in the public sector (Yusoff, 2013).

Performance auditing is a more useful form of environmental auditing for the public sector (Rose, 2001). Public sector auditors tend to consider environmental auditing as performance auditing (Yusoff, 2013). As noted earlier in this chapter, the elements of performance auditing continue to be hotly debated and environmental performance auditing is no exception. Rose (2001) concludes that the focus is more on economy and efficiency, rather than on effectiveness, in meeting environmental objectives as data and methodologies for assessing economy and efficiency are more readily available. Compared with this, the assessment of effectiveness of environmental performance is hindered by the scarcity of data and methodological challenges. Often, environmental objectives are poorly defined, making assessment criteria difficult to formulate. Further, baseline data are rarely available and ecological cause-and-effect relationships are unknown, thus rendering effectiveness difficult to measure (WGEA, 1993, cited by Rose, 2001). While the scarcity of baseline data and long lead times in achieving environmental outcomes are, no doubt, acknowledged factors, broad and non-specific government environmental programme objectives that are difficult to measure, a lack of focus on achieving outcomes and inadequate collection of performance information during implementation (ANAO, 1997) are no less responsible for making assessment of effectiveness difficult.

Environmental auditing is different from the state of environment report and environmental impact assessment/statement

Rose (2001) notes that other methodologies to assess public sector environmental performance – state of environment (SOE) reporting and environmental impact assessment (EIA) – are confused with environmental performance auditing. But they are environmental performance reviews, not performance audits. State of environment reports are scientific 'assessments across a wide range of biophysical and ecological elements of the environment, as well as social and cultural aspects of environmental issues'. In Australia, for example, SOE reporting occurs both at national and state level (DOE, 2015). SOE is largely a scientific assessment of the condition of the environment, not a performance assessment of a government environmental programme or policy. Rose (2001) further observes that while SOE reporting is essential to identifying baseline and changes in environment quality indicators, it does not assess economy, efficiency and effectiveness of any specific public sector commitments. The usual methodology of SOE reporting is the 'Pressure–State–Response' model, whereby it describes the pressures on the environment, the drivers of those pressures, its current condition (state) and the management initiatives or responses undertaken to address environmental concerns, and the impacts of those initiatives (DOE, 2015). State of environment reporting is, thus, a broad picture of environmental condition at a point in time in a continual process that is necessary to develop environmental commitments (policies and programmes) and review them. Unlike environmental auditing, it does not examine the implementation of specific policies and commitments. While SOE reporting may, indirectly, reflect the effectiveness of several environmental initiatives taken by successive governments over time, it does not assess the performance of particular environmental initiatives (Rose, 2001).

The EIA/EIS (environmental impact statement) is required under relevant legislation to be produced by a proponent of a development proposal as a prerequisite for gaining approval (see, for example, §66 of the Australian *Environment Protection and Biodiversity Conservation Act* 1999). While an EIA required before a project is implemented to estimate the future impact of the proposed action, environmental auditing is undertaken after a project has been implemented, or while it is being implemented, to assess the actual impact of the project. So, necessarily, EIA and environmental auditing differ in timing. EIA is at the opposite end of the time continuum from environmental auditing. As noted by He et al. (2009), EIA is an ex-ante assessment, whereas environmental auditing is an ex-post assessment. Environmental auditing can complement an EIA, to assess what impacts actually occurred, and thus ensure that the actual impact remains within the predicted level, and that the condition of approval was adhered to. Environmental auditing, thus, also assesses the performance (effectiveness) of EIA as a management tool (Buckley, 1989). There is also a difference in terms of the actor who actually undertakes the task. EIA is mostly undertaken by public or private sector proponents, or their agents, whereas public environmental audit is undertaken by an SAI (or an equivalent public body). However, some SAIs/audit offices do have mandates to undertake an EIA (WGEA, 1993 cited by Rose, 2001).

Is environmental auditing special?

Generally, the people who conduct environmental auditing in the public sector (SAIs) are of the view that environmental auditing is no different from auditing in other fields and could encompass regularity (financial and compliance) and performance audits (INTOSAI, 2012; Van Leeuwen, 2004; Yusoff, 2013).

Notwithstanding the similarities between environmental audits and audits in other fields emphasized above, panellists at the training session of the Fourteenth Working Group on Environmental Auditing (WGEA) Assembly in November 2011 identified a number of challenges specific to environmental auditing (INTOSAI, 2012).

- Environmental data can often be lacking, diffuse or incomplete at the local, regional and international levels.
- Environmental problems and policy issues are relatively new.
- Sustainability – a core dimension – is fundamentally difficult to address.
- Environmental problems and abatement evolve over the long term.
- Materially linking environmental issues to state finances is a challenge.
- Cost–benefit analysis of the long-term benefits of environmental engagements is crucial but difficult.
- Environmental issues are multinational and interdisciplinary.
- Fieldwork requires specific competencies and knowledge.
- Finding audit criteria on the national level is difficult, but it is also difficult to persuade governments to adopt international criteria.
- Auditing generally has a retrospective focus, but environmental issues require vitality in assessing the potential future impact of policies/programmes.

The WGEA (2012b: 13–14), in its submission to the United Nations Rio+20 conference, identified ten governance problems related to the audit of environment and sustainable development:

- unclear/overlapping responsibilities;
- lack of coordination between subnational levels and the national level;

- absent or deficient policies or strategies;
- insufficient assessment of the environmental effects of governmental policies and programmes;
- lack of analysis (economic, social and environmental) supporting decisions;
- lack of long-term planning to implement environmental policies and programmes;
- inadequate financial management of environmental policies and programmes;
- lack of enforcement of domestic environmental legislation;
- deficient monitoring and reporting systems;
- lack of environmental data for decision making.

Based upon the views of the expert practitioners in the environmental sphere, it can be said that while environmental auditing shares or exhibits the characteristics of an audit, it does have some special characteristics of its own and consequently poses some special challenges. The special place for environmental auditing is also underlined by the fact that of the nine INTOSAI Working Groups, WGEA is the largest (INTOSAI, 2006).

Conclusion

Audit compares 'what is' with 'what should be'. It originated very early in human civilization to hold public officials to account for public money. Audits are of three types – financial, compliance and performance. Performance auditing that deals with economy, efficiency and effectiveness is the most comprehensive form of auditing and largely relates to the public sector. There is an inherent tension between its dual missions of 'accountability' and 'learning'. As opposed to being an internal audit in the private sector describing various types of activities, environmental auditing in the public sector is an 'independent external audit' by SAIs of government programmes and policies dealing with 'environmental issues'. Environmental auditing is no different from auditing undertaken by SAIs in other fields and may comprise one or more of all three types of audit – financial, compliance and performance. However, SAIs acknowledge some specific challenges associated with environmental auditing.

Having introduced the basic concepts of audit and its types and clarified the term environmental auditing, this chapter has prepared for the journey that this book will undertake in subsequent chapters. The next chapter describes global trends in environmental auditing and especially in environmental performance auditing.

References

AASB. (2008). *ASAE 3500*. Melbourne: Auditing and Assurance Standards Board of Australia.

Adams, N. (1986). Efficiency auditing in the Australian audit office. *Australian Journal of Public Administration*, 45(3), 189–200.

ANAO. (1997). *Commonwealth Natural Resource Management and Environment Programs Report No 36 of 1996–97*. Canberra: ANAO.

ANAO. (2014). *Guidelines for the Conduct of Performance Audits*. Canberra: ANAO.

ANAO. (2015a). *Performance Audit Manual*. Canberra: ANAO.

ANAO. (2015b). *Guidelines for the Conduct of Performance Audits*. Canberra: ANAO.

Barrett, P. (2012). Performance auditing: addressing real or perceived expectation gaps in the public sector. *Public Money and Management*, 32(2) 129–136.

Barrett, P. (2015). Trust and confidence in government: whither public audit (unpublished).

Barzelay, M. (1996). Performance auditing and the new public management: changing roles and strategies of central audit institutions. In *Performance Auditing and the Modernisation of Government* (pp. 15–56). Paris: OECD

Barzelay, M. (1997). Central audit institutions and performance auditing: a comparative analysis of organizational strategies in the OECD. *Governance*, 10(3), 235–260.

Behn, R.D. (2001). *Rethinking Democratic Accountability*. Washington, DC: Brookings Institution Press.

Bhandari, C.K. (2014). Engaging civil service organizations in SAI audit. *International Journal of Government Auditing*, 41(2), 24–29.

Blume, L. & Voigt, S. (2007). Supreme audit institutions: supremely superfluous? A Cross Country Assessment: Working Paper No. 3. Mannheim: International Centre for Economic Research.

Bourn, J. (2007). *Public Sector Auditing: Is it Value for Money*. Chichester: John Wiley & Sons.

Bovens, M. (2006). Analysing and assessing public accountability: a conceptual framework. European Governance Papers (EUROGOV), No. C-06-01. Retrieved 20 June 2014 from www.connex-network.org/eurogov/pdf/egp-connex-C-06-01.pdf.

Buckley, R. C. (1989). *Precision in Environmental Impact Prediction: First National Environmental Audit, Australia*. Canberra: Centre for Resource and Environmental Studies, ANU.

Burrowes, A. & Persson, M. (2000). The Swedish management audit: a precedent for performance and value for money audits. *Managerial Auditing Journal*, 15(3), 85–97.

CAG. (2010). *Supreme Audit Institution of India: Brief Introduction*. New Delhi: Comptroller and Auditor General of India.

CAG. (2014). *Performance Auditing Guidelines, 2014*. New Delhi: Comptroller and Auditor General of India.

Daujotait, D. & Mačerinskien, I. (2008). Development of performance audit in public sector. Paper presented at the 5th International Scientific Conference, Vilnius, Lithuania.

DOE. (2015). About State of the Environment (SoE) reporting. Retrieved 25 May 2015 from www.environment.gov.au/topics/science-and-research/state-environment-reporting/about-soe-reporting.

Dye, K. M. (2007). Corruption and fraud detection by supreme audit institutions. In A. Shah (Ed.), *Performance Accountability and Combating Corruption* (pp. 303–321). Washington, DC: World Bank Publications.

Emmett, B. (1996). *Minutes of Proceedings and Evidence of the Standing Committee on the Environment and Sustainable Development, September 17, 1996*. House of Commons, Canada

English, L. M., Guthrie, J., Broadbent, J. & Laughlin, R. (2010). Performance audit of the operational stage of long-term partnerships for the private sector provision of public services. *Australian Accounting Review*, 20(1), 64–75.

Farazmand, A. (1998). Persian/Iranian administrative tradition. In J. Shafritz (Ed.), *International Encyclopaedia of Public Policy and Administration*. (pp. 1640–1645). Boulder, CO: Westview Press.

Finer, H. (1965). Administrative responsibility in democratic government. In F. E. Rourke (Ed.), *Bureaucratic Power in National Politics*. Boston, MA: Little Brown and Company.

Flint, D. (1988). *Philosophy and Principles of Auditing: An Introduction*. Basingstoke: Macmillan Education.

Funkhouser, M. (2008). *Honest, Competent Government: The Promise of Performance Auditing*. Lake Mary, FL: Institute of Internal Auditors Research Foundation.

Funkhouser, M. (2011). Accountability, performance and performance auditing: reconciling the views of scholars and auditors. In J. Lonsdale, P. Wilkins & T. Ling (Eds), *Performance Auditing: Contributing to Accountability in Democratic Government* (pp. 268–288). Cheltenham: Edward Elgar.

Furubo, J. E. (2011). Performance auditing: audit or misnomer? In J. Lonsdale, Wilkins, P. & T. Ling (Eds), *Performance Auditing: Contributing to Accountability in Democratic Government* (pp. 22–50). Cheltenham: Edward Elgar.

GAO. (2011a). *Summary of GAO's Performance and Financial Information*. Washington, DC: GAO.

GAO. (2011b). *Fiscal Year 2012 Performance Plan*. Washington, DC: GAO.

He, G., Zhang, L. & Lu, Y. (2009). Environmental impact assessment and environmental audit in large-scale public infrastructure construction: the case of the Qinghai–Tibet railway. *Environmental Management*, 44(3), 579–589.

Hillary, R. (1998). Environmental auditing: concepts, methods and developments. *International Journal of Auditing*, 2(1), 71–85.

Hodge, G. (2009). Accountability. In P. A. O'Hara (Ed.), *International Encyclopedia of Public Policy* (Vol. 3: Public Policy and Political Economy, pp. 1–17). Perth: Global Political Economy Research Unit.

ICC. (1998). *Environmental Auditing*. Paris: International Chamber of Commerce (ICC) Publishing.

INCOSAI. (1986). General statement on performance audit of public enterprises and audit quality. Paper presented at the International Congress of Supreme Audit Institutions, Sydney.

INTOSAI-ISSAI 3100. (2004). Performance Audit Guidelines: Key Principles. Stockholm: INTOSAI.

INTOSAI. (2004). *Performance Audit Guidelines: ISSAI 3000–3100*. Stockholm: INTOSAI.

INTOSAI. (2006). About us. Retrieved 10 June 2015 from www.intosai.org/about-us.html.

INTOSAI. (2010). Financial Audit Guidelines ISSAI 1000–2999. Stockholm: INTOSAI.

INTOSAI. (2012). Environmental auditing: current and future challenges. *International Journal of Government Auditing*, 39(3), 21–22.

Jones, P. (2008). Audit commission trip to Lithuania. Retrieved 25 March 2015 from www.eurorai.org

Jurado-Sánchez, J. (2002). Mechanisms for controlling expenditure in the Spanish Royal Household, c. 1561-c. 18081. *Accounting, Business & Financial History*, 12(2), 157–185.

Kells, S. (2011). The seven deadly sins of performance auditing: implications for monitoring public audit institutions. *Australian Accounting Review*, 21(4), 383–396.

Kells, S. & Hodge, G. (2009). Performance auditing in the public sector: reconceptualising the task. *Journal of Contemporary Issues in Business and Government*, 15(2), 36–60.

Kelly, J. (1997, 24 November). Watchdog orders end to computer systems row. *Financial Times*.

Lapsley, I. & Pong, C. (2000). Modernization versus problematization: value-for-money audit in public services. *European Accounting Review*, 9(4), 541–567.

Ling, T. (2003). Ex ante evaluation and the changing public audit function the scenario planning approach. *Evaluation*, 9(4), 437–452.

Lonsdale, J. (1999). Impacts. In C. Pollitt, X. Girre, J. Lonsdale, R. Mul, H. Summa & M. Waerness (Eds), *Performance or Compliance? Performance Audit and Public Management in Five Countries* (pp. 171–193). Oxford: Oxford University Press.

Lonsdale, J. (2000). Developments in value-for-money audit methods: impacts and implications. *International Review of Administrative Sciences*, 66(1), 73–89.

Lonsdale, J. (2011). The right tools for the job? Methods, choice and context. In J. Lonsdale, P. Wilkins & T. Ling (Eds.), *Performance Auditing: Contributing to Accountability in Democratic Government* (pp. 95–117). Cheltenham: Edward Elgar.

Lonsdale, J., Ling, T. & Wilkins, P. (2011a). Conclusions: performance audit. An effective force in difficult times? In J. Lonsdale, P. Wilkins & T. Ling (Eds.), *Performance Auditing: Contributing to Accountability in Democratic Government* (pp. 311–336). Cheltenham: Edward Elgar.

Lonsdale, J., Wilkins, P. & Ling, T. (2011b). *Performance Auditing: Contributing to Accountability in Democratic Government*. Cheltenham: Edward Elgar.

Loocke, E. V. & Put, V. (2011). The impact of performance audits: a review of the existing evidence. In J. Lonsdale, P. Wilkins & T. Ling (Eds), *Performance Auditing: Contributing to Accountability in Democratic Government* (pp. 175–208). Cheltenham: Edward Elgar.

Mayne, J. & Schwartz, R. (2005). Assuring the quality of evaluative information. In R. Schwartz & J. Mayne (Eds), *Quality Matters: Seeking Confidence in Evaluation, Auditing and Performance Reporting* (pp. 1–20). Brunswick, NJ: Transaction Publishers.

Morin, D. (2001). Influence of value for money audit on public administrations: looking beyond appearances. *Financial Accountability & Management*, 17(2), 99–117.

Morin, D. (2003). Controllers or catalysts for change and improvement: would the real value for money auditors please stand up? *Managerial Auditing Journal*, 18(1), 19–30.

Morin, D. (2008). Auditors general's universe revisited: an exploratory study of the influence they exert on public administration through their value for money audits. *Managerial Auditing Journal*, 23(7), 697–720.

NAO. (2011). *Annual Report 2011*. London: National Audit Office.

Normanton, E. L. (1966). *The Accountability and Audit of Governments: A Comparative Study*. Manchester: Manchester University Press.

OAG. (2004). *Performance Audit Manual* (pp. 134). Ottawa: Office of the Auditor General of Canada.

Oviir, M. (2012). Environmental auditing in INTOSAI: 20 years later. *International Journal of Government Auditing*, 39(3), 1–5).

Pollitt, C. (1999). Overview. In C. Pollitt, X. Girre, J. Lonsdale, R. Mul, H. Summa & M. Waerness (Eds), *Performance or Compliance? Performance Audit and Public Management in Five Countries* (pp. 194–219). Oxford: Oxford University Press.

Pollitt, C., Girre, X., Lonsdale, J., Mul, R., Summa, H. & Waerness, M. (1999). *Performance or Compliance? Performance Audit and Public Management in Five Countries*. Oxford: Oxford University Press.

Pollitt, C. & Summa, H. (1997). Reflexive watchdogs? How supreme audit institutions account for themselves. *Public Administration*, 75(2), 313–336.

Pollitt, C. & Summa, H. (1999). Performance audit and public management reform. In C. Pollitt, X. Girre, J. Lonsdale, R. Mul, H. Summa & M. Waerness (Eds), *Performance or Compliance? Performance Audit and Public Management in Five Countries* (pp. 1–10). Oxford: Oxford University Press.

Power, M. (1994). *The Audit Explosion*. London: Demos.

Put, V. (2011). Norms used: some strategic considerations from the Netherlands and the UK. In J. Lonsdale, P. Wilkins & T. Ling (Eds), *Performance Auditing: Contributing to Accountability in Democratic Government* (pp. 75–94). Cheltenham: Edward Elgar.

Put, V. & Turksema, R. (2011). Selection of topics. In J. Lonsdale, P. Wilkins & T. Ling (Eds), *Performance Auditing: Contributing to Accountability in Democratic Government* (pp. 51–74). Cheltenham: Edward Elgar.

Quevedo, E. L. (1995). Environmental audit reports: proceed with caution. *Nature Biotechnology*, 13(1), 44–45.

Rika, N. (2009). What motivates environmental auditing? A public sector perspective. *Pacific Accounting Review*, 21(3), 304–318.

Rose, G. (2001). Environmental performance auditing of government: the role for an Australian Commissioner for the Environment. *Environmental and Planning Law Journal*, 18(3), 293–318.

Rubenstein, D. B. (2001). Audit as an agent of constructive consequence and social change. *Corporate Environmental Strategy*, 8(3), 234–241.

Saint-Martin, D. (2004). Managerialist advocate or 'control freak'? The Janus-faced Office of the Auditor General. *Canadian Public Administration*, 47(2), 121–140.

Sartori, G. (1970). Concept misformation in comparative politics. *American Political Science Review*, 64(4), 1033–1053.

Scharaschkin, A. (2011). *Evidence and Argument*. Cheltenham: Edward Elgar.

Shand, D. & Anand, P. (1996). Performance auditing in the public sector: approaches and issues in OECD member countries. In: *Performance Auditing and the Modernisation of Government* (pp. 157). Paris: OECD.

Stern, E. (2005). Auditing for social change in the context of the Millennium Development Goals. Paper presented at the 6th Global Forum on Reinventing Government Towards Participatory and Transparent Governance.

Summa, H. (1999). Definitions and frameworks. In C. Pollitt, X. Girre, J. Lonsdale, R. Mul, H. Summa & M. Waerness (Eds), *Performance or Compliance? Performance Audit and Public Management in Five Countries* (pp. 11–29). Oxford: Oxford University Press.

Sutherland, S. L. (2003). 'Biggest scandal in Canadian history': HRDC audit starts probity war. *Critical Perspectives on Accounting*, 14(1), 187–224.

Suzuki, Y. (2004). Basic structure of government auditing by a supreme audit institution. *Government Auditing Review*, 11, 39–53.

UN/INTOSAI. (2011). 21st UN/INTOSAI Symposium on Effective practices of cooperation between Supreme Audit Institutions and citizens to enhance public accountability. Paper presented at the UN/INTOSAI Symposium,13–15 July, Vienna, Austria,.

UN/INTOSAI. (2013). 22nd UN/INTOSAI Symposium on audit and advisory by SAIs: risks and opportunities, as well as possibilities for engaging citizens. Paper presented at the UN/INTOSAI Symposium, 5–7 March, Vienna, Austria.

Van Leeuwen, S. (2004). Developments in environmental auditing by supreme audit institutions. *Environmental Management*, 33(2), 163–172.

WGEA. (2001). *Guidance on Conducting Audit of Activities with an Environmental Perspective*. The Hague: WGEA.

WGEA. (2007). *Evolution and Trends in Environmental Auditing INTOSAI Working Group on Environmental Auditing*. The Hague: WGEA

WGEA. (2012a). About environmental auditing. Retrieved 24 March 2014 from http://environmental-auditing.org/Home/LearningCentre/AboutEnvironmentalAuditing/tabid/122/Default.aspx

WGEA. (2012b). *Improving National Performance: Environmental Auditing Supports Better Governance and Management*. Stockholm: INTOSAI.

WGEA. (2013). *Auditing Water Issues: An Examination of SAIs' Experiences and the Methodological Tools They Have Successfully Used*. Stockholm: INTOSAI.

Wighton, D. (1998, 8 January). NHS rapped for delay to report. Financial Times.

Wilkins, P. & Boyle, R. (2011). Standards and quality. In J. Lonsdale, P. Wilkins & T. Ling (Eds), *Performance Auditing: Contributing to Accountability in Democratic Government* (pp. 147–171). Cheltenham: Edward Elgar.

Yusoff, H. N. (2013). Understanding environmental audit in the public sector: Malaysian perspective. *Jurnal Teknologi*, 62(1), 25–30.

3 Global trends in environmental performance auditing

This chapter describes global trends in environmental auditing and especially in environmental performance auditing. Trends have been investigated through an analysis of the initial two decades (1992–2012 – a period considered sufficient for trend analysis) of global data on environmental auditing publicly available from the International Organization of Supreme Audit Institutions (INTOSAI) Working Group on Environmental Auditing (WGEA) website (www.environmental-auditing.org). The WGEA is one of the nine (and largest[1]) working groups of INTOSAI – the global professional organization of Supreme Audit Institutions (SAIs). Established in 1953, INTOSAI is a non-governmental organization (NGO) with special consultative status with the Economic and Social Council of the United Nations. It provides an institutional framework to SAIs for promoting the development and transfer of knowledge, capacity building and professional enhancement of government auditing worldwide. Within INTOSAI, there are seven regional groups that promote its goals (INTOSAI, 2006):

OLACEFS: Organization of Latin American and Caribbean Supreme Audit Institutions;
AFROSAI: African Organization of Supreme Audit Institutions;
ARABOSAI: Arab Organization of Supreme Audit Institutions;
ASOSAI: Asian Organization of Supreme Audit Institutions;
PASAI: Pacific Association of Supreme Audit Institutions;
CAROSAI: Caribbean Organization of Supreme Audit Institutions; and
EUROSAI: European Organization of Supreme Audit Institutions.

INTOSAI (2006) also has a number of committees, working groups, and task forces. The INTOSAI committees deal with issues of significant, recurring interest to all members of INTOSAI – for example, preparing standards and guidelines. Working groups deal with specific themes and publish specific guidance and best practices. INTOSAI established the WGEA in 1992 with a mission to assist SAIs in better undertaking of environmental auditing; to facilitate the exchange of information and experience between SAIs; and to publish guidelines and other information for their use (WGEA, 2012b).

A key line of investigation here is whether the socio-economic conditions of a country influence environmental performance auditing by its SAI. The answer may appear obvious to some. However, an objective analysis is considered necessary to confirm this assumption. This analysis has been undertaken with the help of socio-economic data (such as per capita gross national income (GNI) and developmental status of countries) from the World Bank website (https://data.worldbank.org). A description of SAIs' mandate is given before presenting the results of relevant trend analysis in the subsequent sections.

Audit mandate

Mandate refers to the powers of SAIs to conduct audits. It determines the type of audits (e.g. financial, compliance or performance) an SAI can undertake, and the types of bodies (such as national government, state government, non-government organizations) it can audit. A manifestation of audit mandate is the power to access or seek information. The reach of SAIs or the level of access to information to different types of bodies can also determine the audit tools an SAI can use in its work (WGEA, 2012a: 10). The mandate of SAIs varies significantly from one country to another, depending upon the type of governing structure (federal, unitary), the type of democracy (parliamentary, presidential) and legal and political history and associated traditions. Mandate relates to all matters SAIs can audit; however, the discussion here is in the specific context of the audit of environmental matters.

Key statistics on SAIs' mandates are given in Table 3.1.

Types of audit

The majority of SAIs can conduct performance audits (92–94 per cent), compliance audits (90–91 per cent) and financial audits (85–88 per cent) in relation to environmental matters. About one-third of SAIs also have the power to conduct *a-priori* audits. About one-fifth of SAIs have a specific mandate for auditing environmental matters. For example, the Auditor General of Canada, through the Commissioner of the Environment and Sustainable Development (CESD) reporting to him or her, has a specific mandate for conducting audit of matters related to the environment and sustainable development. Established in 1995, the CESD: monitors sustainable development strategies of the Canadian federal departments; oversees the environmental petitions process; and audits the federal government's management of environmental and sustainable development issues (OAG, 2014). There are 26 other SAIs that have a specific mandate for auditing environmental matters. The OLACEFS (seven) region has the highest number of SAIs having a specific mandate for environmental auditing followed by AFROSAI (six) and EUROSAI (six).

Supreme Audit Institutions have been debating whether a specific mandate is needed to undertake environment audits (WGEA, 2007a: 23). However, they have come to the view that a specific environment audit mandate is not

Table 3.1 SAI mandate analysis

Particular	*WGEA website (percentage of SAIs)*			*WGEA seventh survey (2012) (percentage of SAI)*		
Data	N = 131 (64%)			N = 112 (62%)		
1. Mandate: types of audit						
Financial	85			88		
Compliance	90			91		
Performance	92			94		
A priori	33			32		
Specific reference to environment	21			19		
2. Mandate: extent	**Full access (%)**	**Partial access (%)**	**No access (%)**	**Full access (%)**	**Partial access (%)**	**No access (%)**
National government	95	5	0	94	3	3
State/provincial or regional government	70	18	12	70	17	13
Local/municipal or community government	70	17	13	68	17	15
State-owned enterprises	79	17	4	82	13	5
Semi-government organizations	44	44	12	48	43	9
Non-governmental public enterprises or organizations	12	41	47	13	44	43
Private sector organizations	1	35	65	2	33	65

Part 1 of the table relates to the types of audits; part 2 to the types of bodies SAIs can audit.

necessary for undertaking environmental audits (WGEA, 2004:ii; 2007a: 23; 2012a:11). Despite this, a small percentage of SAIs in their survey responses consider an inadequate mandate as a barrier to environmental auditing (for example, in the seventh survey (WGEA, 2012a: 69), overall 11 per cent of SAIs report it as a barrier). While the framework of a specific mandate for environmental auditing has changed very little over time, the volume of environmental auditing has been growing (see next section). This may be due to SAIs becoming more aware of the ways in which they can use their traditional mandate to examine environmental programmes and policies (WGEA, 2012a: 8).

Extent of mandate

Most SAIs (Table 3.1) have full access (power to seek information) to the national government (94–95 per cent), provincial or regional government (70 per cent), local/municipal or community government (68–70 per cent) and state-owned enterprises (79–82 per cent). About half (44–48 per cent) have full access to semi-government organizations. As environmental issues often involve multiple levels of government, they are often audited at multiple levels. The extensive audit mandate of many SAIs gives them the opportunity to assess how all levels of government are working to protect the environment (WGEA, 2007b: 10).

Access to non-governmental public enterprises or organizations (12–13 per cent) and private sector organizations (1–2 per cent) is limited. The majority of SAIs either have partial or no access to these organizations. Partial access in these cases likely means that SAIs can only inspect the use of public money allotted to these organizations (WGEA, 2012a: 11) in some restricted manner. This may be problematic for some SAIs in undertaking environmental audits, as the mandate would not give access to all bodies involved in the environmental policy administration. This means that the SAIs would need to get part of the information required for audit from bodies outside their mandate on a voluntary basis. As such information could not be made public, the SAIs in their audit reports would need to limit themselves to the bodies in their mandate, 'thus presenting only a part of the actual situation' (Van Leeuwen, 2004). Barrett (Former Auditor General of Australia, personal communication), however, considers that SAIs could publish such information in a 'non-confidential' aggregate manner.

Limiting SAIs' access to non-government and private sector organizations is likely to have growing implications for environmental auditing in the future. The involvement of the private sector in the provision of public services, including the delivery of environmental programmes, has been growing (see for example, Dobbs and Pretty, 2008; Jellinek et al., 2013; Stobbelaar et al., 2009). Non-governmental organizations are already involved in delivery of environmental programmes in several countries. For example, Sulabh International, an NGO, is extensively involved in providing sanitation services in India. To ensure transparency and accountability, limited SAIs' access to these organizations would need to be addressed in future. The so-called doctrine of 'follow the public money' could be invoked to address this issue.

Environmental audits have been growing

The number of both total environmental audits and environmental performance audits has been growing (Figure 3.1). This figure also shows that environmental performance audits closely follow the time pattern of total environmental audits. This is expected as a growing proportion of environmental audits are performance audits. Over the two-decade period 1992–2012, globally SAIs produced 3,654 environmental audit reports. The first decade (1,793 or 49 per cent) and the second decade (1,861 or 51 per cent) each produced about half of total environmental audits. Of the total 3,654 environmental audits, a larger proportion (2,372 or 65 per cent) were performance audits. The first decade produced 813 and the second decade 1,559 environmental performance audits. The average proportion of environmental performance audits was higher in the second decade (84 per cent) than in the first decade (46 per cent).

Total environmental audits peaked at 300 reports per year in 1996. Following some troughs and peaks in the intervening period, it reached another, lower, peak of about 270 per year in 2008. After a steep fall from 2008, the growth in environmental audits seems to have plateaued around 2009. Figure 3.1 shows that the environmental audits and environmental performance audits are broadly related to global economic conditions, reflected by global average gross domestic product (GDP). As the global GDP increases, so do environmental audits and environmental performance audits, and vice versa. For example, plateauing out of the growth in environmental audits around 2009 is plausibly related to the global financial crisis (GFC) that generally constrained public finances everywhere. SAIs, while independent in most cases, still depend upon governments' budgetary allocation for their functioning, and thus are not immune to financial shocks felt by national economies. A further investigation found that the trend lines of environmental performance audits and that of global GDP were parallel, confirming a close relation between the two. This is plausible, as growth in annual average GDP is a broad indicator of the global economic conditions that determine the globally averaged capacity to spend on governmental programmes

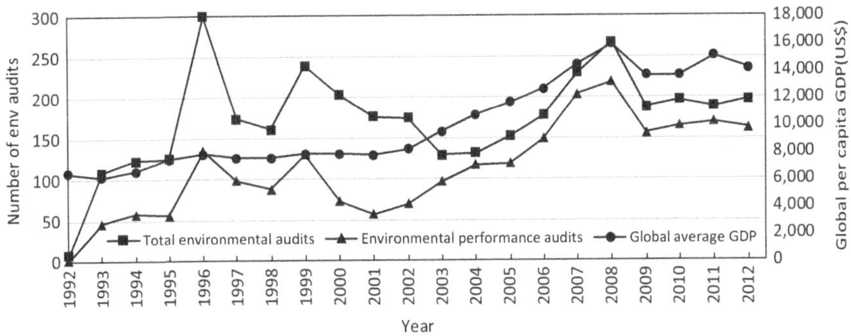

Figure 3.1 Global environmental audits and environmental performance audits during 1992–2012.

Source: after Prasad, 2018.

generally, on environmental programmes particularly, and also on the budgets of SAIs.

Overall, despite some peaks and troughs and plateauing in later years, there is an increasing trend in environmental audits and in environmental performance audits. The growth in environmental audits is a result of both the increasing number of SAIs undertaking environmental audits each year and the increasing number of audits undertaken by SAIs each year that are already active in environmental auditing. The data show that the number of SAIs that produced at least some environmental audits in a year has been increasing. The number of SAIs undertaking environmental audits increased from 6 in 1992 to 66 in 2007, and dropped off to 55 in 2012. The number of SAIs undertaking environmental performance audits increased from 1 in 1992 to 62 in 2011, dropping to 51 in 2012.

Risks to public expenditure and the operation and performance of public administration play a key role in the selection of audit topics by SAIs (Put and Turksema, 2011). The increase in environmental policies and programmes and associated expenditure globally (Keene and Pullin, 2011) means an increase in such risks. It is, therefore, expected that a growing number of SAIs would be prompted to undertake more and more environmental audits.

Proportion of environmental performance audits and compliance audits

The percentage of environmental performance audits as a proportion of total environmental audits has mostly been increasing (Figure 3.2). Amid some intermittent peaks and troughs, it increased from 13 per cent in 1992 to 82 per cent in 2012. Despite a downturn during 1999 to 2001, overall the percentage of performance audits increased six-fold between 1992 and 2012. The sharp dip in the proportion of performance audits during 2000–2002 (Figure 3.2) seems somewhat unusual. This may be related to the change in the WGEA audit classification system (WGEA has different classifications for pre- and post-2003 environmental

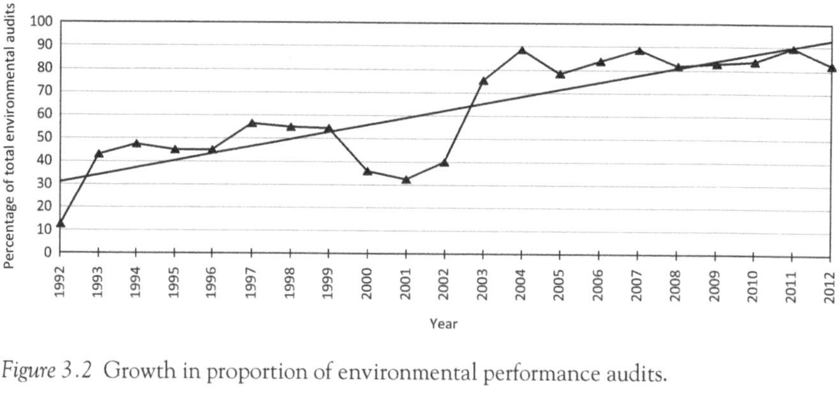

Figure 3.2 Growth in proportion of environmental performance audits.

audits). In anticipation of the new classification system, SAIs might have slowed down reporting (wait and watch) and in order to spend some efforts in learning the proposed system.

Unlike the data for environmental performance audits that were available for the whole 1992–2012 period, the data for compliance audits were available only for the 2003–2012 period. A comparison between the two for the common period showed that compared with performance audits, the percentage of compliance audits decreased. While the percentage of performance audits increased from 75 per cent to 82 per cent, the percentage of compliance audits dropped from 67 per cent to 42 per cent during this period.

The growth in the percentage of performance audits underlines the increasing importance of performance audits in environmental matters. This suggests that economy, efficiency and effectiveness of the implementation of environmental policies and programmes are considered increasingly more important than just compliance with environmental laws and policies. It is consistent with the long-held view that compliance does not always mean effectiveness (see, for example, Faure and Lefevere, 1999). As performance auditing is a much broader concept than regularity auditing, it generally requires more resources (Van Leeuwen, 2004). Therefore, growth in environmental performance audits would suggest that SAIs are investing belatedly more resources in these audits.

Uneven growth in environmental performance audits

Regional distribution of environmental performance audits

The geographical distribution of environmental performance audits (Table 3.2) indicates that Europe (975, 41 per cent) is the largest contributor to global

Table 3.2 Regional distribution of environmental performance audits (EPAs) and of SAIs with nil EPAs for the period 1992–2012

	SAIs population	*EPAs*	*Nil-EPA-SAIs*	*SAI (%)*	*EPA (%)*	*Nil-EPA-SAIs (%)*
Europe	44	975	9	21	41	9
South America	12	369	4	6	16	4
Asia	30	299	13	15	13	13
North America	2	296	0	1	12	0
Central America	8	121	3	4	5	3
Africa	55	119	39	27	5	38
Middle East	16	111	9	8	5	9
South Pacific	16	79	4	8	3	4
Caribbean	22	3	21	11	0	21
Total	205	2,372	102	100	100	100

Source: after Prasad, 2018.

environmental performance audits, followed by South America (369, 16 per cent), Asia (299, 13 per cent) and North America (296, 12 per cent) in the next three spots. Central America (121, 5 per cent), Africa (119, 5 per cent) and the Middle East (11, 5 per cent) are in the fifth, sixth and seventh spots respectively. The South Pacific, with 79 audits (3 per cent), is in the eighth spot while the Caribbean region, with three environmental performance audits, is in the last spot.

The number of SAIs in each region does not explain the volume of environmental performance audits. Africa, with the largest share of global SAIs (55, 27 per cent), accounts for only 5 per cent of the global environmental performance audits, whereas North America, with only 1 per cent of the global SAIs population, accounts for 12 per cent of global environmental performance audits. It may be noted that the North American region comprises only two countries: the United States of America (USA) and Canada, which are among the world's wealthiest nations. Naturally, their SAIs would be among the most resourceful. On the other hand, the African region is home to the world's poorest countries, with their SAIs likely to have the fewest resources. The same can also be said about the Caribbean region. This suggests a potential relationship between the SAI's parent country's economic development and the number of environmental performance audits undertaken. The existence of a potential relationship between economic factors and the output of environmental performance audits is further strengthened by the concentration of 102 SAIs (fourth column of Table 3.2) that have not undertaken environmental performance audits in the world's poorer regions. The highest concentration of SAIs that have not undertaken environmental performance audits (the last column of Table 3.2) during 1992–2012 is in Africa (38 per cent), followed by those in the Caribbean (21 per cent).

In terms of economic development, of the 102 SAIs that did not produce any environmental performance audits, 84 (82 per cent) belong to developing countries and 18 (18 per cent) to developed countries. The region (Africa) that is most lagging in environmental performance audit also has the highest number of low-income countries. In Africa, low-income countries outnumber middle- and high-income countries. This would suggest that the capacity of an SAI could be related to its parent country's level of economic development. However, regions other than Africa (Table 3.2), have more countries in high- and middle-income brackets than in low-income brackets. This may suggest that there could be some income threshold below which income level becomes the sole determinant of capacity and beyond which other factors (e.g. environmental awareness) also play a role.

Frequency distribution of environmental performance audits

The global distribution of performance audits is skewed (Figure 3.3). For the period 1992–2002, 75 per cent of SAIs (154 countries) contributed little to the global total of environmental performance audits. Cumulatively, about 90 per cent of SAIs (185 countries) produced about 15 per cent of environmental

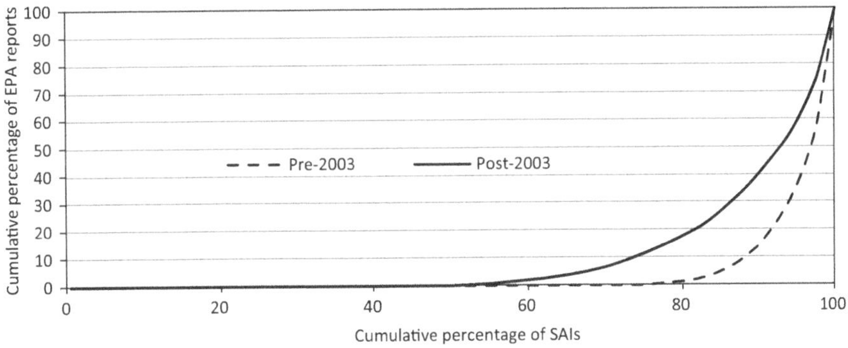

Figure 3.3 Cumulative percentage of environmental performance audits (EPAs) versus cumulative percentage of SAIs.

Source: after Prasad, 2018.

performance audits. About 97 per cent of SAIs (199 countries) produced about half (52 per cent) of environmental performance audits; the top 3 per cent of SAIs (six countries) produced about the remaining half (48 per cent) of environmental performance audits. The top 2 per cent of countries (four) produced 35 per cent of total environmental performance audits. Overall, the top ten countries produced 63 per cent of total environmental performance audits (813) during 1992–2002.

For the period 2003–2012 (Figure 3.3), about 50 per cent of SAIs (102 countries) made nil contribution to global environmental performance audits. Cumulatively about 75 per cent of SAIs (154 countries) produced about 12 per cent of environmental performance audits. About 93 per cent of SAIs (190 countries) produced about half (49 per cent) of environmental performance audits; the top 7 per cent of SAIs (15 countries) produced about the remaining half (51 per cent) of environmental performance audits. The top 2 per cent (four) of countries produced about 20 per cent of total environmental performance audits. Overall, the top ten countries produced 40 per cent of environmental performance audits (1,559) for the period 2003–2012.

Even after 20 years since this record has been maintained, about half of SAIs not undertaking any environmental performance audits is a significant issue. This may indicate capacity constraints in SAIs and other barriers (discussed in Chapter 6) such as a lack of environmental policies or programmes, or at least auditable environmental policies or programmes in these countries.

Notwithstanding a large proportion of SAIs not conducting environmental performance audits, there has been significant progress in this regard. The progress in global environmental performance audits has been both in terms of magnitude and distribution. Compared with the first decade (813), the number of environmental performance audit reports almost doubled (1,559) in the second decade. Further, more SAIs conducted environmental performance audits during the second decade than in the first decade. The proportion of SAIs that did not conduct any EPA declined from 75 per cent in the first decade to 50 per cent in the second decade (Figure 3.3). This implies that about 50 more SAIs conducted an environmental performance audit in the second decade than in the first decade.

The area between the dotted line curve and the solid line curve in Figure 3.3 denotes the additional participation of SAIs during the post-2003 decade. The increase in participation of SAIs in environmental performance audits is a welcome sign of progress. As an audit requires the involvement of both an auditor and an auditee, this progress reflects progress on the part of both parties. General global progress, including growth in income and standard of living, spread of education, increase in environmental awareness/consciousness and a consequent increase in environmental policies and programmes, may be some of the causal factors attributable to the auditees.

Increase in awareness and willingness to enhance transparency and the accountability of governments towards the public and increase in the capacity of SAIs to undertake environmental performance audits may be some causal factors attributable to auditors. These causal factors may not be exclusive; rather, they may be more likely to be common. These factors may be reduced to economic factors, such as capacity of governments to spend on environmental programmes and environmental factors such as environmental awareness in the SAIs. Again, there may not be a clear dividing line between economic and environmental factors. For example, the capacity of SAIs to undertake environmental performance audits may be related to both economic (budget) and environmental (skills) factors.

Country's income level and its output of environmental performance audits are related

The relationship between the average per capita national income (1992–2012) of individual countries that produced some environmental performance audits and their output of environmental performance audits (1992–2012) was investigated. This showed generally an increasing trend in environmental performance audits with an increase in national income. However, no definite conclusions could be drawn about an individual country's national income and its output of environmental performance audits as the relationship was largely variable. Countries' outputs of environmental performance audits (e.g. Australia (45) and Canada (135)) with similar national incomes were significantly different. Factors other than purely economical ones might be at play in the conduct of environmental performance audits, making a general conclusion at an individual country level about a country's environmental performance auditing capacity based purely on its national income not possible. However, when an aggregation is made at a higher level, the factors that cause individual differences between similar entitles are smoothed out and the dominant characteristics of the aggregated group become more prominent. This led to the investigation of the relationship between an SAI's parent country's income level – high, medium, low (World Bank, 2014) – and their output of environmental performance audits as a group (here, note that

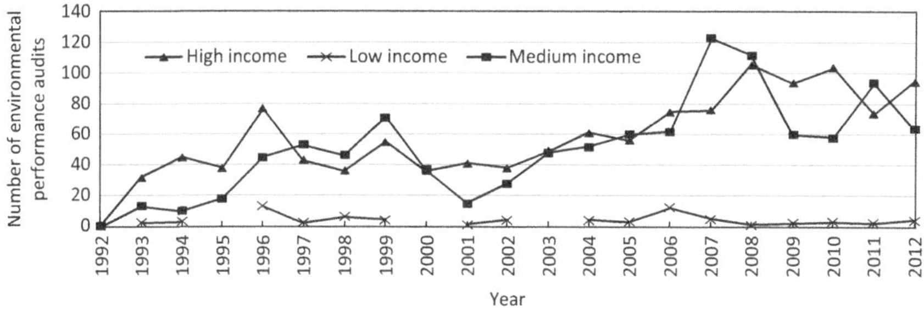

Figure 3.4 Relationship between the income level of SAIs' parent country and environmental performance audits.

Source: after Prasad, 2018.

high-income countries are described as developed countries and middle-income and low-income countries together as developing countries).

The middle-income and high-income countries produced more environmental performance audits than the low-income countries (Figure 3.4). As discussed earlier, the environmental performance audits may be related to a country's capacity to spend on environmental programmes as well as its SAIs' capacity to undertake performance audits of those programmes. Both of these factors in some way are related to a country's national income. Therefore, it is expected that low-income countries would produce fewer performance audit reports than would middle and high-income countries.

The middle-income countries seem to occasionally overtake the high-income countries in undertaking environmental performance audits after 1997. They outperform the high-income countries except during some downturn periods, such as a few years post-1999 and post-2008. Both of these periods mark some major economic events – the first is the Asian economic crisis and the second is the GFC. There is also more volatility in the trend of middle-income countries, compared with that of high-income countries. The greater number of middle-income countries than high-income countries would suggest that, as a group, the former would have more environmental programmes than the latter. Lonsdale et al. (2011: 313) observe that some of the growth in performance audits generally, in these countries, has been stimulated by donor agencies such as the World Bank and Asian Development Bank. Unlike low-income SAIs, middle-income SAIs may reasonably be sometimes more resourceful compared with their high-income peers. Therefore, the middle-income SAIs occasionally producing more environmental performance audits than high-income SAIs is not inconsistent with expectations.

The middle-income SAIs fall below their high-income counterparts in 2009, rise above them in 2011, only to fall slightly below them in 2012. As may be expected, middle-income countries would have less resilience to weather the GFC of 2008–2009 than did high-income countries. It is highly likely that in middle-income countries, SAIs would have faced harsher restrictions on their budgets (reducing their capacity to undertake performance audits generally, and particularly in the environmental domain, which is generally not of high priority in these countries) than their counterparts in high-income countries. Less resilience in middle-income SAIs is further evidenced by the fact that they take two years to turn around/recover post-GFC, compared with only one year taken by high-income SAIs. The lower resilience of middle-income SAIs is also shown by the fact that they were affected almost immediately in 2008 (when the GFC hit), whereas their high-income peers were affected two years later.

When middle- and low-income countries are grouped together as developing countries and compared with high-income (developed) countries, the overall contrast seen between high-income and middle-income countries in Figure 3.4 continues, and becomes more pronounced. Middle-income countries are already occasionally outperforming the high-income countries. While the low-income countries have an overall decreasing trend in environmental performance audits, adding their results to the middle-income countries will further increase the existing difference with high-income (developed) countries. Barring some major world economic downturn periods, developing country SAIs, as a group, tend to outperform their developed peers post-1996 for the reason discussed above. However, it should be noted that overall, during 1992–2012, developed SAIs produced more environmental performance audits (see discussion in the paragraph below) than their developing peers, suggesting their greater resources and hence capacity to do so.

Over the two-decade period 1992–2012, globally, developing country SAIs (1,983) produced more total environmental audits than their developed country peers (1,671). However, during the same period, the former (1,140) undertook fewer environmental performance audits than the latter (1,232). As performance auditing is a much broader concept than regularity auditing, it generally requires more resources (Van Leeuwen, 2004). From this perspective, it may be concluded that the developing country SAIs, as a group, have fewer resources and capacity to undertake environmental performance audits than their developed country peers.

WGEA membership and the output of environmental performance audits are related

The WGEA member countries have always produced more environmental performance audits than non-member countries (Figure 3.5). It is further evident from this figure that the difference between the WGEA member countries and non-member countries is increasing post-2003. The WGEA member countries seem to have recovered from the GFC downturn within a year and continue to increase the number of their environmental performance audits. However, for non-member countries, despite a slight recovery, the downturn continues. Other factors responsible for this shift cannot be ruled out. However, a strong correlation between the WGEA membership and countries' overall output of environmental performance audits is clear.

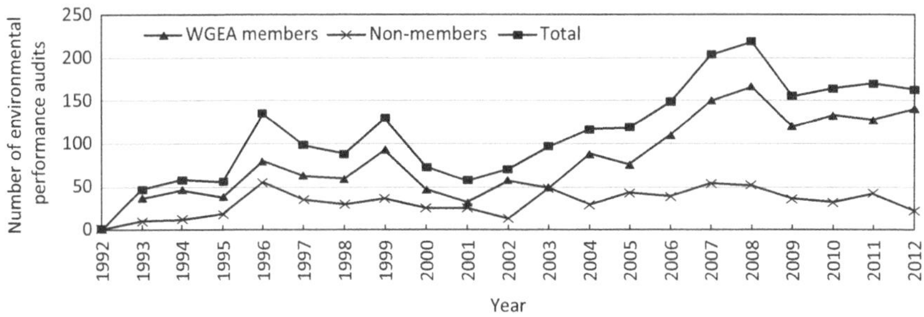

Figure 3.5 Environmental performance audits by WGEA member and non-member countries.

Source: after Prasad, 2018.

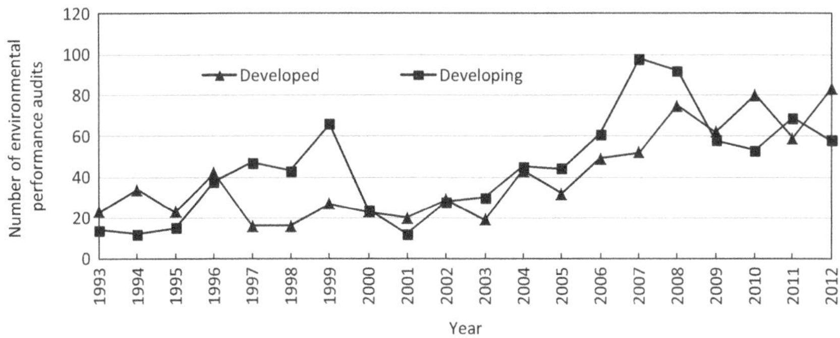

Figure 3.6 Environmental performance audits of WGEA member countries grouped into developed and developing countries.

Source: after Prasad, 2018.

The effect of WGEA membership becomes more revealing when the results for WGEA members and non-members are further subdivided into development categories. The WGEA member developing countries mostly outperform their developed peers (Figure 3.6). In contrast to this, barring a few exceptions, developed non-WGEA member countries outperform their developing peers (Figure 3.7).

The influence of the membership on the conduct of environmental performance audits seems to be so strong that it can compensate for, and thus prevails over, the obvious incapacity/barrier caused by economic factors. The association with the WGEA increases the awareness and enhances the skill set of SAIs required to undertake environmental performance audits (see for example, WGEA, 2012a: 32). These factors perhaps have a stronger influence on the ultimate output of environmental performance audits than resources alone that may be available because of higher economic level of SAIs. The results here

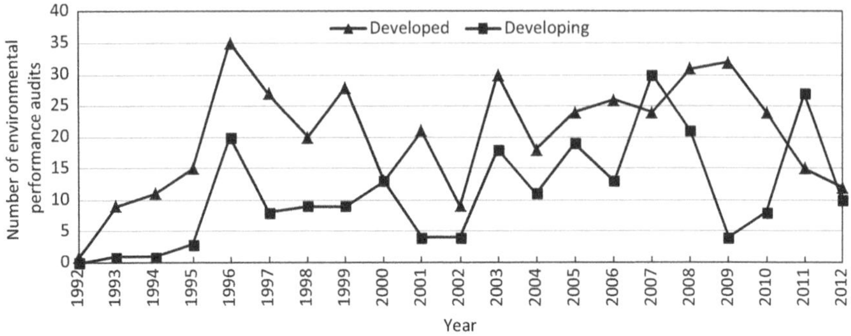

Figure 3.7 Environmental performance audits for WGEA non-member countries grouped into developed and developing countries.

Source: after Prasad, 2018.

clearly indicate that the WGEA (2012c) is succeeding in its aims to improve the use of audit mandate and the audit process in the field of environmental protection policies, by both WGEA member and non-member SAIs. The growth in environmental audits is a measure of its success. However, not surprisingly, member SAIs seem to have benefited more than non-member SAIs.

While countries/SAIs that are active in environmental auditing are also likely to become members of the WGEA, the membership seems to have a catalytic effect on SAIs in terms of their output of environmental audits. SAIs that are members of the WGEA have more opportunities to network. Hence, they are more likely to learn from the experience of fellow member SAIs. Thus, they are more likely to undertake environmental performance audits of emerging issues, knowing how others have done it. Overall, it could be argued that environmental awareness/consciousness of SAIs evident through their activities in environmental auditing, and their membership of the WGEA, reinforce each other. Therefore, WGEA members produce more environmental audits than non-members.

Issues in global environmental performance audits

The environmental policies and programmes cover a broad range of issues. Consequently, environmental performance audits also cover a wide range of issues. The WGEA has categorized issues in pre- and post-2003 environmental audits differently. However, as issue categorization is more structured and comprehensive for the post-2003 period, audit issues for this period are more amenable to analysis than for the pre-2003 period.

Issues in post-2003 environmental performance audits

The WGEA has catalogued the post-2003 environmental audits into 8 main issues and 77 sub-issues. The main issues and some key sub-issues covered in

Table 3.3 Main issues and key sub-issues in global environmental performance audits during 2003–2012

Main issue	*Key sub-issues (WGEA categories)*	*Number of environmental performance audits*
Air		**365**
	Climate change	142
	Local air quality, such as smog, particulates, SO_2, NO_x, CO_2	105
	Toxic air pollutants, such as organic POPs, dioxins, furans	45
Ecosystem		**893**
	Biodiversity	162
	Protected areas and natural parks	158
	Ecosystem management and ecosystem changes	139
Governance		**1,388**
	Environmental management system	323
	Domestic funds and subsidies	284
	Environmental impact assessment	225
	Sustainable development	186
Human activities and sectors		**1,318**
	Environment and human health	197
	Energy and energy efficiency	175
	Infrastructure	174
Natural resources		**338**
	Forestry and timber resources	118
	Fisheries (freshwater and marine)	84
Waste		**660**
	Municipal, solid, non-hazardous waste	146
	General waste	141
	Hazardous waste	134
Water		**739**
	Pollution of water bodies (such as by industry and agriculture)	183
	Wastewater treatment	149
	Drinking water – quality and supply	142
Other		**116**
Grand total		**5,817**

environmental performance audits are listed in Table 3.3. In the main issues category, governance (1,388), human activities and sectors (1,318) and ecosystem (893) emerge as the top three main issues, followed by water (739), waste (660) and air (365).

Many of the main category issues may not be independent. Some of them, for example governance, may be a cross-cutting issue. Some issues, like human activities and sectors, may have overlap with some others. For example, agriculture and pesticides may overlap with the water sub-issue-pollution of water bodies (such as by industry and agriculture). The overlap is evidenced by the fact that in 1,559 environmental performance audit reports post-2003, 5,817 issues are covered. This gives an average of about four issues per environmental performance audit. Compared to the 1992–2002 period (about two issues per performance audit), the issue coverage has almost doubled. This indicates an increase in complexity and comprehensiveness of environmental performance audits that has significant implications for capacity and capability of SAIs. However, it should be noted that two periods use different classification of issues. Given the developments in performance auditing, it is possible that complexity of environmental performance audits would have grown. However, this remains a hypothesis that needs to be tested by analysing the complexity within the same period.

Governance emerges as the top category of main issues, with 1,388 environmental performance audits. This should not be surprising as performance auditing, despite some reservations (see, for example, Kells and Hodge, 2009) is about economy, efficiency and effectiveness of public policy implementation (INTOSAI-ISSAI, 2004: 1) and governance lies at the centre of these matters. As such, governance may be a cross-cutting theme across the performance audit of most other environmental issues, such as ecosystem, air, water and waste, and therefore gets the highest count of performance audits. This argument may also apply to the second highest main category of issue, human activities and sectors, due to its potential overlap with other issues such as air, water and waste.

Physical environmental issues, such as water (739), waste (660), biodiversity (162) and climate change (142) are quite prominent audit issues among SAIs. These matters are of significant public importance, due either to their critical nature (e.g. water and waste) or to enhanced public concern, because of their salience and topicality resulting from greater awareness (e.g. climate change and biodiversity). As these matters attract greater attention in public policies and resultant public investments, they become issues of interest to SAIs. Additionally, in several countries, executive or legislature (such as in the USA) may request their SAI to conduct performance audits of matters important to them. Therefore, the matters that have greater public importance get more attention from SAIs than matters that are of less interest to the public or their representatives. The WGEA (2012e) has made some of these matters of high public importance the focus of its activities and has produced guidelines to help SAIs conduct relevant performance audits.

An analysis of the top 20 individual issues identified suggests that they (3,477 issues) accounted for about 60 per cent of total coverage of issues (5,817 in Table 3.3). The cross-cutting governance-related issues (mostly socio-economic development), such as environmental management system (323), domestic funds and subsidies (284), and environmental impact assessment (225) have received the greatest attention. Apart from financial matters (domestic funds and subsidies), the presence of environmental management systems and environmental impact assessments among the top three issues underlines the importance of environmental governance, including monitoring, reporting and accountability systems. SAIs' selection of audit topics generally reflects governments' and communities' priorities and concerns, which will vary between countries. However, a trend in globally aggregated values does indicate that environmental governance is globally highly important.

The next three individual issues are environment and human health (197), sustainable development (186), and pollution of water bodies (183). Climate change (142) ranks fourteenth on the global ranking of issues, though a related issue, energy and energy efficiency (175) is in seventh position, much higher in ranking. The emergence of sustainable development as the fifth top global issue is interesting. The concept of 'development that meets the needs of the present generation without compromising the ability for future generations to meet their own needs' (WCED, 1987) was put forward in the late 1980s. Gradually, it has gained acceptance and currency in the public and private sectors. It is now a major consideration in government planning and policy making (WGEA, 2007a: 15). About one-quarter of SAIs reported in the fifth survey (WGEA 2007a: 15) that they were already conducting audits of sustainable development programmes.

An investigation of temporal variation of the top 20 issues found that generally there was a peak during the 2006–2008 period. Some global events, such as the debate over carbon accounting (Barrett, personal communication) may have influenced auditing of other environmental issues. However, this matter needs further investigation.

The coverage of issues is related to a country's economic development

The coverage of issues in environmental performance audits seems to be related to countries' economic development, as can be seen from the inclusion of the top ten issues for high-income (developed) countries (Table 3.4); middle-income countries (Table 3.5); and low-income countries (Table 3.6). For the high-income (developed) countries (Table 3.4), the top three issues were: (1) domestic funds and subsidies; (2) environmental management system; and (3) energy and energy efficiency. Climate change was the fourth most important issue; sustainable development took the fifth spot before infrastructure and environment and human health; and ecosystem management and ecosystem changes took the tenth spot.

For the middle-income countries (Table 3.5), the top three issues were: (1) environmental management system; (2) environmental impact assessment; and (3) pollution of water bodies (such as by industry and agriculture). Domestic funds and subsidies was the next most important issue; environment and human health took the fifth spot and sustainable development the sixth, ahead of protected areas and natural parks as well as wastewater treatment. The last two

Table 3.4 Top ten issues in post-2003 environment performance audits for high-income countries

Ranking	*Issue type/ category(WGEA categories)*	*Issue (WGEA categories)*	*Number of environmental performance audits*
1	Governance	Domestic funds and subsidies	206
2	Governance	Environmental management system	155
3	Human activities and sectors	Energy and energy efficiency	148
4	Air	Climate change	134
5	Governance	Sustainable development	99
6	Human activities and sectors	Infrastructure	98
7	Governance	Other governance issues	96
8	Human activities and sectors	Environment and human health	89
9	Ecosystems	Biodiversity	88
10	Ecosystems	Ecosystem management and ecosystem changes	82

Source: after Prasad, 2018.

Table 3.5 Top ten issues in post-2003 environment performance audits for middle-income countries

Ranking	*Issue type/ category(WGEA categories)*	*Issue (WGEA categories)*	*Number of environmental performance audits*
1	Governance	Environmental management system	200
2	Governance	Environmental impact assessment	156
3	Water	Pollution of water bodies (such as by industry and agriculture)	118
4	Governance	Domestic funds and subsidies	109
5	Human activities and sectors	Environment and human health	108
6	Governance	Sustainable development	107
7	Ecosystems	Protected areas and natural parks	98
8	Water	Wastewater treatment	93
9	Waste	General waste	91
10	Waste	Municipal, solid, non-hazardous waste	88

Table 3.6 Top ten issues in post-2003 environment performance audits for low-income countries

Ranking	*Issue type/ category(WGEA categories)*	*Issue (WGEA categories)*	*Number of environmental performance audits*
1	Waste	Municipal, solid, non-hazardous waste	9
2	Natural resources	Forestry and timber resources	8
3	Water	Drinking water – quality and supply	8
4	Waste	Hazardous waste	7
5	Human activities and sectors	Infrastructure	5
6	Governance	Sustainable development	4
7	Waste	General waste	4
8	Governance	Agriculture	3
9	Ecosystems	Biodiversity	3
10	Water	Water quantity management or management of watersheds	3

spots were taken by general waste, and municipal, solid and non-hazardous waste. Interestingly, climate change did not find a place in the top ten issues.

For the low-income countries (Table 3.6), the top three issues were: (1) municipal solid (non-hazardous) waste; (2) forestry and timber resources; and (3) drinking water. Hazardous waste was in fourth place, ahead of infrastructure; sustainable development was in sixth place, followed by yet another waste issue – general waste. Water quantity management or management of watersheds took the tenth spot (note that agriculture and biodiversity also have identical numbers of reports). Again, climate change did not figure in the top ten issues.

A pattern in the issues of importance is discernible here. The lower the income/economic development level, the more important are development and sustenance issues, and quality issues such as governance and air quality slide down in importance; and vice versa. This is consistent with expectations, as developed countries have already addressed the developmental issues in the past, whereas developing countries are still dealing with them. Domestic funds and subsidies, which is the top issue for high-income (developed) countries, is the fourth issue of importance for developing middle-income countries; it does not find a place in the top ten issues for low-income countries. Climate change, which is the fourth top issue of importance for developed countries does not find a place in the top ten issues for developing countries. Municipal solid (non-hazardous) waste is the top issue for low-income countries, whereas it is the last issue for middle-income country SAIs and does not appear in the most important ten issues for high-income SAIs. This finding may be significant for INTOSAI when considering assistance for capacity building (e.g. training) for middle- and low-income (developing) countries.

Objectives of environmental performance audits

Performance auditing is a broad concept (Van Leeuwen, 2004) that examines a government entity's economy, efficiency and effectiveness in performing its functions and activities, not excluding the entity's compliance with applicable laws and regulations. As such, the objective(s) of an environmental performance audit may encompass a range of government responsibilities, including compliance with the relevant environmental laws, policies and agreements, as well as performance of audited entities in implementing the government's environmental policies and programmes, the so-called three Es: economy, efficiency and effectiveness.

Objectives of pre-2003 environmental performance audits

The WGEA catalogues the objectives of pre-2003 environmental audits into the following eight categories (the abbreviations in brackets are used in Figure 3.8 due to space limitations):

- performance audit of environmental policies (PA env policy);
- performance audit of the implementation of environmental programmes (PA env prog);
- evaluate impacts or effects of existing national environmental programmes (Eval env prog);
- evaluate impacts or effects of proposed national environmental programmes (Eval prop prog);
- audit environmental effects of non-environmental programmes (Env effect of non-env);
- audit compliance with national environmental laws and regulations by government departments, ministries and/or other bodies (Comp nat env laws);

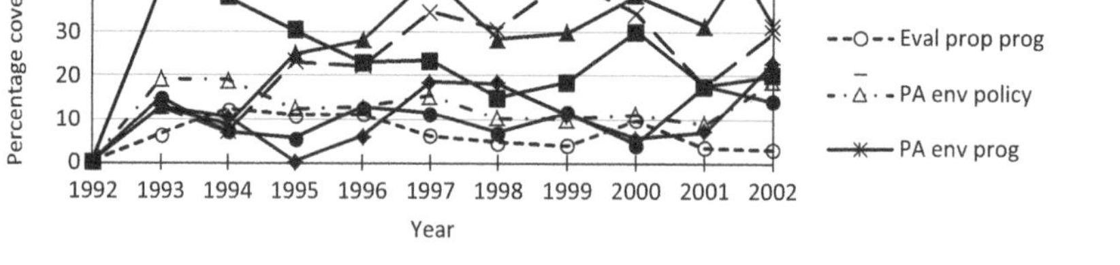

Figure 3.8 Temporal variation of proportion of each objective in pre-2003 global environmental performance audits.

- audit compliance by the government with international obligations and commitments the government has signed (Comp int env laws); and
- audit government environmental management systems (Env mgmt sys).

An analysis of audit objectives data for this period finds that 813 performance audits had 1,498 objectives, giving a ratio of about two (1.8) objectives per performance audit. Of the 813 performance audits, 482 audits – the largest proportion (59 per cent) – have performance audits of the implementation of environmental programmes as an objective, followed by 254 audits (31 per cent) that have compliance with national environmental laws and regulation as an objective. Audits of government environmental management systems take third place, appearing in 225 (28 per cent) audits, followed by evaluating impacts of existing national environmental programmes that appears in 195 audits (24 per cent). Performance audit of environmental policies appearing in 107 audits (13 per cent); audit of environmental effects of non-environmental programmes in 92 audits (11 per cent); and audit of compliance with international obligations in 86 audits (11 per cent) take the next three spots. Evaluating impacts or effects of proposed national environmental programmes appears as an objective in the least number of audits at 57 (7 per cent).

The coverage of objectives in performance audits demonstrates their relative importance to SAIs. As the audit type itself is a performance audit, performance examination of some sort is expected more than any other objective. However, it is interesting to note that not all environmental performance audits have this objective. In the pre-2003 period, performance audit of environmental policies was considered as a separate objective. Even when this is separately accounted for, except in 1992, not all performance audits have examination of performance as an objective.

Identifying or defining suitable audit criteria for performance examination of environmental programmes and policies and associated systems and processes is a challenging endeavour. Despite some headway, it remains a work in progress. The period being considered is the very beginning of environmental performance auditing. So, a lesser proportion of performance audits (amid growing volume), not having some sort of performance examination, is quite reasonable. As the aggregated data do not indicate where (which region, which income group) it was happening, it may need further investigation to understand the causes.

The temporal trend in objectives was as expected – as the number of performance audits increased, the count of each objective increased and vice versa. However, the trend in performance audit of the implementation of environmental programme objective after 2001 was an exception. It did not follow the increasing trend in environmental performance audits after 2001. Existence of a similar but separate objective – performance audit of environmental policies – may partly explain the decreasing trend. When the proportion of the environmental performance audits having this objective as a percentage of total environmental performance audits is considered (Figure 3.8), the performance audit of the implementation of environmental programme audit objective is seen to have a decreasing trend, even after ignoring the initialization effect (starting in one out of one audit). While existence of a similar objective (performance audit of environmental policies) might partly explain this decreasing trend, it is possible to have other explanations. This may also suggest that SAIs had a bit of catching up to do. While more environmental performance audits were being conducted and more had performance audits of the implementation of environmental programmes as an objective, a progressively lesser proportion of total environmental performance audits listed this objective. It is possible that newer SAIs that were adding to the growing volume of performance audits were not yet including performance examination as an objective.

Objectives of post-2003 environmental performance audits

The WGEA catalogues objectives of post-2003 environmental audits into the following seven categories (the abbreviations in brackets are used in Figure 3.9 due to space limitations):

- fair presentation of financial statements and expenditures (Fin audit);
- compliance with international environmental agreements (Comp int laws);
- compliance with domestic environmental legislation (Comp dom leg);
- compliance with domestic environmental policies (Comp dom pol);
- performance of government environmental policies and programmes (PA env pol&prog);
- environmental impacts of non-environmental government programmes (Env imp of non-env); and
- evaluate environmental impacts of proposed environmental policies and programmes (Eval prop prog).

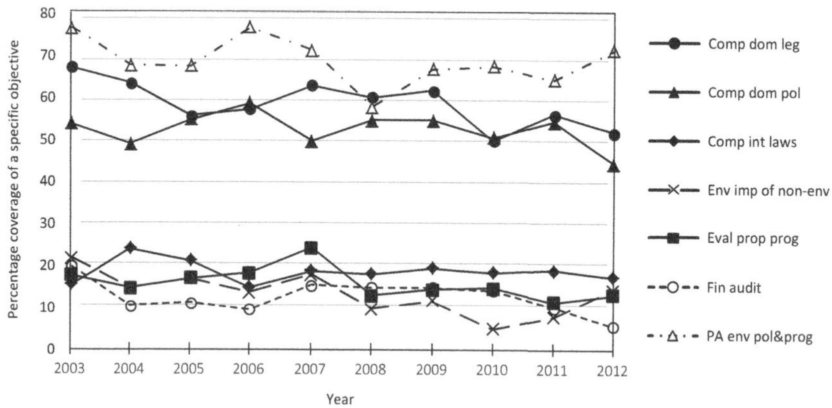

Figure 3.9 Temporal variation of proportion of each objective in post-2003 global environmental performance audits.

An analysis of objectives of post-2003 environmental performance audits indicated that 1,559 performance audits had 3,698 objectives, giving a ratio of more than two (2.4) objectives per performance audit. The increase in this ratio compared with that in the pre-2003 period (1.8) may suggest an increase in the complexity and sophistication of environmental performance audits.

Of the 1,559 performance audits, 1,058 audits – the largest proportion (68 per cent) – have performance of government environmental policies and programmes as an objective, followed by 906 audits (65 per cent) that have compliance with domestic environmental legislation as an objective. Compliance with domestic environmental policies takes third place, appearing in 813 (58 per cent) audits followed by compliance with international environmental agreements that appears in 287 audits (18 per cent). Evaluating environmental impacts of proposed environmental policies and programmes appears in 244 audits (16 per cent) and environmental impacts of non-environmental government programmes in 197 audits (13 per cent), taking the next two spots. Fair presentation of financial statements and expenditures appeared in 193 audits (12 per cent) and takes the last position.

Compared with the pre-2003 period, the coverage of all comparable objectives increased. Overall, this possibly suggests increasing complexity of performance audits in the post-2003 period. Note that the performance of government environmental policies and programmes that were separate objectives pre-2003 were merged together by the WGEA post-2003, while compliance with environmental laws and regulations that was a single objective pre-2003 was split into two objectives – compliance with domestic environmental legislation and compliance with domestic environmental policies. Fair presentation of financial statements and expenditures was added, while audit of environmental management systems was dropped.

There was little unexpected temporal trend in objectives: as the number of performance audits increased, the number of each objective increased and vice versa. However, the temporal variation of proportion of objectives of performance audits (Figure 3.9) is quite interesting, especially when compared with the pre-2003 variation (Figure 3.8). The contrast between the two groups of objectives-performance of domestic policies and programmes and compliance with domestic environmental legislation, on the one hand, and evaluating environmental impacts of proposed environmental programmes and non-environmental policies and programmes, on the other, is sharper in the post-2003 period (Figure 3.9) than in the pre-2003 period (Figure 3.8). While in the later part of the pre-2003 period the coverages of these two groups of objectives are very close to each other, they are far apart throughout the post-2003 period. This shows that SAIs have settled for a greater focus on performance and compliance objectives in the post-2003 period than on evaluation of impact objectives.

The pre-2003 declining trend in the proportion of the performance of government environmental policies and programmes objective has drastically changed in the post-2003 period. Compared with a 43-point decline in the coverage of this objective from 74 per cent in 1993 to 31 per cent in 2002 (ignoring the high initial value of 1992) in the pre-2003 period, there is only a decline of 5 points from 76 per cent in 2003 to 71 per cent in 2012. If the initial value of 2003 is ignored, there is an increase of 3 points from 68 per cent in 2004 to 71 per cent in 2012. Merging of two similar objectives – performance of environmental programmes and performance of policies – might explain some differences. However, the trend suggests that there is some basic shift in the coverage of the performance objective. The merging of two similar objectives in itself is significant in that it underlines the challenges in separating the examination of performance (effectiveness) of environmental programme implementation from the effectiveness of performance of policies. The debate in the performance audit literature about the examination of effectiveness of outcome of policies versus the examination of effectiveness of processes of implementation of policies is far from settled, as noted in Chapter 2. Notwithstanding this merger of policies and programmes effectiveness and the related debate, the increase in the coverage of performance objectives compared to the pre-2003 period, and steady to increasing trend post-2003, indicates a marked shift. Post-2003, a high proportion of about 70 per cent (and higher than the pre-2003 period of about 60 per cent) of performance audits examined the performance of environmental policies and programmes. This also shows growing confidence and maturity of SAIs in not only conducting performance audits, but also developing tools and techniques for examining performance of environmental policies and programmes.

Joint/cooperative audits

Encouraging joint auditing by SAIs is part of the WGEA mission (WGEA, 2012d). Such audits are helpful, especially for the audit of cross-border environmental issues and policies, and the audit of international environmental agreements. Through these audits, SAIs can exchange information, train each other, build capacity and network with each other. They can also compare (benchmark) results and audit findings with other countries, making their audit reports stronger. Benchmarking is particularly appealing to parliamentarians, who like to know how the laws and policies they make perform compared with those of other countries (WGEA, 2007a: 16). While cooperation between SAIs occurs on a range of matters, cooperation on the audit of implementation of multilateral environmental agreements (MEAs) and audit of transboundary issues is more prominent.

The WGEA (1998: 10–16) describes three types of cooperative audits: concurrent (parallel), joint and coordinated audits. In concurrent audits, SAIs choose a common audit topic and exchange ideas and experiences. However, they simultaneously undertake their own audits with separate audit teams, and produce their own report for their respective legislature/government. In a joint audit, SAIs form a single team of auditors from all the participating countries, which conducts the audit together and produces a joint audit report that is published in all the participating countries. The coordinated audit may be a joint audit with separate reports (as in the concurrent audit), or concurrent audits with a joint report in addition to separate national reports. In the trend analysis discussed here, the three types of audits together have been referred to as joint audits

During the period 2002–2012, a total of 46 joint environmental audits were conducted by a total of 201 participant countries (note that these are not 201 individual countries, but a grand total of the number of countries that participated in joint audits each year). This gives an average of four countries per joint/cooperative audit. However, the average needs to be considered carefully. There is a large variation in the number of countries participating in a cooperative joint audit. The minimum number of participant countries in a cooperative audit is obviously two. The maximum number of SAIs that participated in a cooperative audit during 2002–2012 was 17. Sixty-four individual countries participated in these cooperative audits. Fifty-two countries were involved in 1–4 joint audits; eight countries were involved in 5–8 joint audits; one country each in 9–12 and 13–16 joint audits; and only two countries were involved in 17–20 joint audits.

The Russian Federation (18) has participated in the maximum number of joint audits, followed by Poland (17), Ukraine (15), Norway (9) and the Slovak Republic (8). It is interesting to note that most of these top-performing countries were either from, or were aligned with, the former Union of Soviet Socialist Republics (USSR). In terms of income and developmental levels, 48 per cent of participants in cooperative audits were high-income SAIs; 51 per cent middle-income SAIs; and only 1 per cent were low-income SAIs (48 per cent developed and 52 per cent developing country SAIs). As with the individual audits, this again reflects the severe limitations that low-income SAIs face in conducting cooperative environmental audits. The higher participation of middle-income SAIs in cooperative audits is consistent with their higher activities in environmental audits (as discussed earlier). In terms of geographical regions, most of the participating countries came from Europe (75 per cent) and the South Pacific (9 per cent). The regional dominance of Europe is partly explained by the continued historical cooperation between the former Soviet republics. Further, Europe has been more active than other regions in terms of regional and global cooperation on environmental initiatives.

Types of audits in cooperative/joint audits

Except for two years (2006 and 2008), joint audits were always performance audits. Overall, 96 per cent (44 of 46) of joint environmental audits were performance audits, 76 per cent were compliance audits and only 28 per cent were financial audits (as an audit can simultaneously be of more than one type, their total percentage may exceed 100). As joint audits are mostly concerned with audit of implementation of multilateral environmental agreements or transboundary issues, they would intuitively be expected to be more concerned with compliance. However, the results indicate that the performance of governments, for example in achieving targets, is considered more important than just complying with the rules. If the effect of initialization (starting with a very low initial value in 2002 and then growth) between 2002 and 2003 is ignored, the overall trend in compliance audit is downwards. This is consistent with the trend in individual audits discussed earlier. The decreasing trend in compliance audit should not be interpreted as a decrease in interest in compliance. SAIs choose audit topics and types of audit largely based upon assessed risks. The decrease in compliance audits only means that SAIs see compliance as a lesser risk than, for example, performance that is invariably considered to have a higher level of risk.

Issues in joint/cooperative audits

Altogether, 229 issues were covered in 46 audits. This is an average of five issues per audit report. Compared with the coverage of issues in individual audits (four), issue coverage of joint audits is higher. When several SAIs work together on a joint audit, it is possible that more issues would need to be considered so that each country's needs are served. In terms of the main categories of issues, governance comes at the top with its coverage in 62 audit reports followed by ecosystems (56), water (38) and waste (19). Of the main categories of issues, air (14) is covered in the fewest audits, trailing human activities and sectors (18) and natural resources (15). As discussed earlier, the highest coverage of governance issues is due to their cross-cutting nature. The ecosystem-related issues, such as biodiversity, coastal areas, protection of marine habitat, rivers and lakes and wetlands have resulted in greater cooperation among SAIs than do air-related issues such as climate change and acid precipitation. Of the ten top individual issues, the top four, environmental management system (17), ecosystem management and ecosystem changes (13), protected areas and natural parks (11) and biodiversity (11) are ecosystem-related issues.

While air-related issues are also transboundary, there are more global and regional treaties and agreements on ecosystem-related matters than for air-related matters. This can also be said about water-related issues such as marine pollution. Perhaps also, issues related to ecosystem, water, waste (such as municipal and solid waste), human activities and sectors (such as agriculture and natural disaster management) and natural resources (e.g. fisheries, forestry and timber resources) are more immediate issues, attracting public attention, and hence are of more currency and importance to SAIs than air-related issues. Therefore, these issues appear in a greater number of cooperative audits.

Objectives of joint/cooperative audits

Compliance with domestic environmental legislation (80 per cent) as an objective was equally prevalent as compliance with international environmental agreements (80 per cent) in joint audits. It may seem counter-intuitive in that cooperative audits are about matters of mutual interest to all participating SAIs, so joint/international matters should get prominence over domestic matters. However, this is not inconsistent with actual practice. Generally, countries enact domestic legislation to implement international environmental agreements and treaties, so compliance with an enabling domestic legislation will result in compliance with the relevant international agreement. The next most prominent objective is performance of government environmental policies and programmes (78 per cent). This shows that a focus on performance (e.g. achievement of targets and systems and processes associated with them) is very high on the priority list of SAIs. This is a very encouraging sign for international environmental initiatives.

Conclusion

Globally, environmental performance audits have been growing in number and possibly in complexity. However, the growth has been uneven. About half of SAIs have not produced any environmental performance audits, suggesting capacity gaps. These SAIs are largely concentrated in Africa and the Caribbean – two economically poor regions. Both a country's economic development and its membership of the WGEA are correlated to its output of environmental performance audits. Economic factors influence the choice of audit topics. Generally, the developed country SAIs focus on performance auditing of quality-of-life environmental issues, such as climate change, whereas developing country SAIs concentrate on subsistence environmental matters such as water supply and sanitation.

Having stepped through the theoretical foundations of auditing in the previous chapter and trends in environmental performance auditing here, the next chapter will investigate current practices in environmental performance auditing.

Note

1 As of September 2017,WGEA has 79 members (WGEA, 2017)

References

Dobbs, T. L. & Pretty, J. (2008). Case study of agri-environmental payments: the United Kingdom. *Ecological Economics*, 65(4), 765–775.

Faure, M. & Lefevere, J. (1999). Compliance with international environmental agreements. In S. Axelrod, J. D. L. Down, N. J. Vig (Eds), *The Global Environment Institutions, Law And Policy*, (pp. 138–156). Washington, DC: CQ Press.

INTOSAI-ISSAI. (2004). Performance Audit Guidelines: Key Principles. Stockholm: INTOSAI.

INTOSAI. (2006). About us. Retrieved 10 June 2015 from www.intosai.org/about-us.html.

Jellinek, S., Parris, K. M., Driscoll, D. A. & Dwyer, P. D. (2013). Are incentive programs working? Landowner attitudes to ecological restoration of agricultural landscapes. *Journal of Environmental Management*, 127, 69–76.

Keene, M. & Pullin, A. S. (2011). Realizing an effectiveness revolution in environmental management. *Journal of Environmental Management*, 92(9), 2130–2135.

Kells, S. & Hodge, G. (2009). Performance auditing in the public sector: reconceptualising the task. *Journal of Contemporary Issues in Business and Government*, 15(2), 36–60.

Lonsdale, J., Ling, T. & Wilkins, P. (2011). Conclusions: performance audit – an effective force in difficult times? In J. Lonsdale, P. Wilkins & T. Ling (Eds), *Performance Auditing: Contributing to Accountability in Democratic Government* (pp. 311–336). Cheltenham: Edward Elgar.

OAG (2014). Who we are. Retrieved 23 July 2014 from www.oag-bvg.gc.ca/internet/English/au_fs_e_370.html#Commissioner.

Prasad, A. (2018). Global trends in performance auditing of environmental policies and programs: implementation. *Journal of Sustainability Science and Management*. In press.

Put, V. & Turksema, R. (2011). Selection of topics. In J. Lonsdale, P. Wilkins & T. Ling (Eds), *Performance Auditing: Contributing to Accountability in Democratic Government* (pp. 51–74). Cheltenham: Edward Elgar.

Stobbelaar, D. J., Groot, J. C., Bishop, C., Hall, J. & Pretty, J. (2009). Internalization of agri-environmental policies and the role of institutions. *Journal of Environmental Management*, 90, S175–S184.

Van Leeuwen, S. (2004). Developments in environmental auditing by supreme audit institutions. *Environmental Management*, 33(2), 163–172.

WCED (1987). Our Common Future. New York: WCED, United Nations

WGEA. (1998). *How SAIs May Co-operate on the Audit of International Environmental Accords*. Stockholm: INTOSAI Working Group on Environmental Auditing.

WGEA. (2004). *Fourth Survey on Environmental Auditing*. Stockholm: INTOSAI Working Group on Environmental Auditing.

WGEA. (2007a). *Fifth Survey on Environmental Auditing*. Stockholm: INTOSAI Working Group on Environmental Auditing.

WGEA. (2007b). *Evolution and Trends in Environmental Auditing*. Stockholm: INTOSAI Working Group on Environmental Auditing.

WGEA. (2012a). *Seventh Survey on Environmental Auditing*. Stockholm: INTOSAI Working Group on Environmental Auditing.

WGEA. (2012b). About environmental auditing. Retrieved 24 March 2014 from http://environmental-auditing.org/Home/LearningCentre/AboutEnvironmentalAuditing/tabid/122/Default.aspx.

WGEA. (2012c). *Improving National Performance: Environmental Auditing Supports Better Governance and Management*. Stockholm: INTOSAI Working Group on Environmental Auditing.

WGEA. (2012d). About WGEA. Retrieved 15 August 2014 from http://environmental-auditing.org/Home/AboutWGEA/MissionandMandate/tabid/102/Default.aspx

WGEA. (2012e). Home. Retrieved 12 September 2014 from http://environmental-auditing.org.

WGEA. (2017). Message from the chair. *Greenlines*, 18(2). Retrieved 18 November 2017 from www.environmental-auditing.org/media/5317/eng17pu_green18n2sep.pdf.

World Bank. (2014). How does the World Bank classify countries? Retrieved 12 July 2014 from https://datahelpdesk.worldbank.org/knowledgebase/articles/378834-how-does-the-world-bank-classify-countries.

4 Current practices in environmental performance auditing

Based upon a global survey of Supreme Audit Institutions (SAIs), this chapter discusses the current practice (i.e. the state of the craft) in environmental performance auditing, such as the selection of environmental topics for auditing, methods used for evidence collection, framing of audit criteria and the standard and guidelines used for quality assurance of audits. Both their objective response and their views on different matters have been captured. A further point of investigation is how SAIs' practices are influenced by the developmental status of their parent country. The survey was conducted with the assistance of the Working Group on Environmental Auditing (WGEA). The target participant group was made up of the 107 SAIs (75 developing and 32 developed countries)[1] that had experience in undertaking environmental performance audits. These SAIs were identified primarily by the analysis of global data on environmental audit, discussed in Chapter 3. The overall response to the survey was 45 per cent. The response rate of developed SAIs (56 per cent) was higher than that of developing SAIs (40 per cent). Responding to a survey consumes resources without any immediate tangible benefit. Expectedly, the developed countries' SAIs, with generally more resources, are more likely to respond than their developing country peers with fewer resources.

Strategic planning and selection of environmental matters for performance audit

Strategic audit planning

Environmental matters feature in almost all SAIs strategic planning, suggesting that they have entered the mainstream of performance auditing at least in the strategic sense. However, whether this strategic intent is translated into real audits would depend upon many factors, including immediate priority vis-à-vis available audit resources. The WGEA's three-yearly work plan (WGEA, 2012) has considerable influence over the strategic planning of SAIs – more so on developing SAIs (about half) than developed SAIs (about one-third). This is consistent with Rika's (2009) observation that international bodies such as the UN and WGEA exert more influence on developing countries than on developed countries. The WGEA's three-year work plan is a product of active deliberation among WGEA members. More developing SAIs than developed SAIs benefiting from it suggests that the developing SAIs, as a group, are net receivers of benefits of the WGEA three-year planning. This is a positive sign of influence of the WGEA.

Topic selection

Some SAIs (about 20 per cent) that have a specific mandate over environmental matters would necessarily choose environmental matters for annual performance auditing, with the selection being limited to which environmental topic to audit. However, for the vast majority of SAIs, environmental topics compete with other topics, such as health and education. Generally, SAIs choose topics using the following methods:

- structured approach that considers matters such as risks involved in programmes, materiality and salience of issues;
- sectoral approach, in which environmental matters are picked up as per their relative importance; and
- request by the legislature or other stakeholders.

An overwhelmingly large proportion (94 per cent) of SAIs indicates (Figure 4.1) using a structured approach to choosing a topic for environmental performance audit. A large proportion (44 per cent) also indicates taking a sectoral approach, in

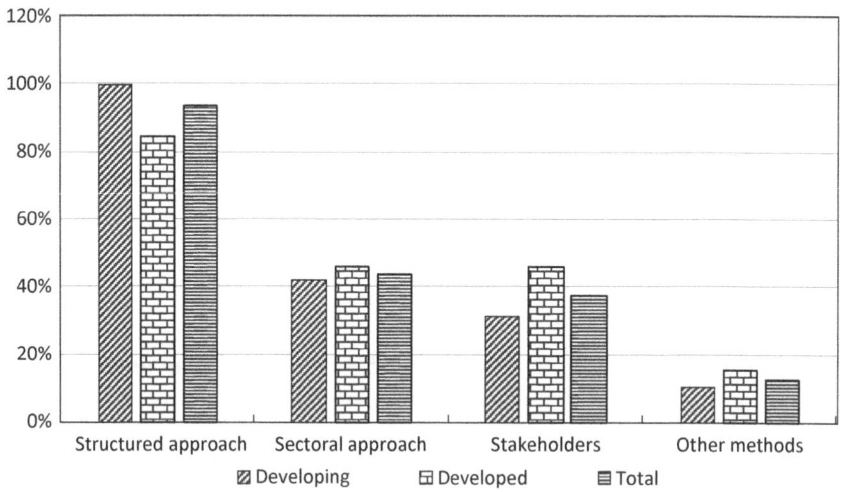

Figure 4.1 How do you select the environmental matters for performance audit from among all other matters (e.g. health, education): (a) structured approach; (b) sectoral approach: (c) stakeholders' request; and (d) other methods? Response (percentage) of SAIs that have do not have specific mandate for environmental audit – developing SAIs (N = 19); developed SAIs (N = 13); total SAIs (N = 32).

which environmental matters are selected as per their relative importance. About one-third or more of SAIs indicate selecting an environmental audit topic based upon requests by stakeholders (e.g. parliamentarians, government). This is consistent with expectations. While SAIs are generally independent in their choice of audit topics, they do consider stakeholders' requests in the selection of audit topics. Independence does not preclude consideration of stakeholders' requests, it only means that they are not bound by such views. A small proportion (6–13 per cent) of SAIs indicated using methods other than those specified as options. These other methods included approaches such as: (1) balancing between small and larger audits, new and follow-up audits and consideration of auditing resources; and (2) selecting audits mandated by law.

Compared with developed SAIs, developing SAIs report a higher use of a structured approach and a lower use of stakeholders' request. The lower use by the developed SAIs of a structured approach (85 per cent) seems to be compensated by their higher proportion of the use of the sectoral approach, stakeholders' requests and other methods. A higher use of stakeholders' requests by developed SAIs than the developing SAIs in this group is consistent with the expectation of a more consultative governance in developed countries than in developing countries. As SAIs reflect the prevailing norm within the state machinery of their country (Pollitt and Summa, 1997), this would mean that developed SAIs would be more consultative than their developing peers.

Some common phrases used to describe topic selection by both groups of SAIs (with and without explicit environmental audit mandate) are: 'multi-year strategic planning', 'risk analysis of key domains of government activities', 'relevance', 'likely impact', 'previous audit findings', 'auditability', 'stakeholder (mainly legislative authorities) interest', 'materiality', 'complexity', 'significance', 'visibility (media, legislation and citizen)', 'past coverage', 'cross sectoral' and 'public interest'. Some SAIs note that the environment is one of their 'priority' areas. One SAI observes that most of its environmental audits are in 'response to requests from the legislature' and some are 'mandated by law'. The following two observations of SAIs, one with and one without an explicit environmental audit mandate, aptly summarize the process of topic selection.

1 We perform a systematic evaluation on risk areas annually. Relevant topics for audits are based on risk and materiality (economic and other). All of the departments (Performance/Financial) at all levels in the organization is involved in this process. Our mandate also opens [us] to perform audits based on request from the Parliament, but such requests are very rarely received.
2 We have a multiannual audit strategy, combined with annual priorities. Topics are selected following a structured approach based on such issues as our assessment of risk, relevance, likely impact, previous audit findings, auditability, and stakeholder (mainly legislative authorities) interest. Potential audit tasks are subject to a quality review by a central service of [our SAI] which compares the proposal with [our SAI's] strategy and annual priorities. We also consider available audit resources.

Proportion of environmental audits

The percentage of environmental performance audits as a proportion of total performance audits can indicate the relative importance of an SAI's environmental performance audit work. A little more than two-thirds of SAIs indicate that environmental performance audit work is 10 per cent or less of their total performance audit work, while the remaining (about one-third) SAIs indicate it is 11 per cent or more. The largest proportion of SAIs (34 per cent) indicate that environmental performance audits comprise 6–10 per cent of their total performance audit work, whereas the second largest (30 per cent) proportion of SAIs indicate it is 2–5 per cent. Only a small proportion (5 per cent) of SAIs indicate that their environmental performance audit work is 1 per cent or less of their total performance audit work. On the higher side, 16 per cent of SAIs indicate that their environmental performance audit work is 11–20 per cent and another 16 per cent indicate that it is 20 per cent or more. The overall message emerging from the results is that environmental performance audit is significant but still a small (10 per cent or less) proportion of the total performance audit work for more than two-thirds of SAIs.

Criteria for environmental performance audits

Audit criteria are reasonable and attainable standards of performance against which the economy, efficiency and effectiveness of activities or operations are assessed. They can be derived from official/authoritative sources (e.g. policy, legislation) or non-authoritative sources (INTOSAI, 2004: 135) – i.e. developed by an SAI on its own by research of relevant literature or using international norms (Put, 2011). INTOSAI (2004: 104) considers it useful to get input from auditee(s) in developing criteria. However, recognizing that disagreements may exist, it suggests their identification, and resolution if possible (INTOSAI, 2004: 104).

Consultation with auditee in developing audit criteria

The majority of SAIs (57 per cent) indicate (Figure 4.2) that they develop criteria for environmental performance audit in consultation with auditees. However, audit criteria are also developed independently and auditees are only informed by 43 per cent of SAIs.

A higher proportion of developing country SAIs (65 per cent) than developed country SAIs (44 per cent) appear to be constructing criteria for environmental performance audit in consultation with auditees. Conversely, a higher proportion of developed SAIs (56 per cent) than developing SAIs (35 per cent) seem to develop audit criteria independently of auditees. This appears somewhat inconsistent with expectations as, compared with developing countries, SAIs in developed countries are expected to be more consultative, reflecting the broader trend of governance (Pollitt and Summa, 1997). It is possible that given the

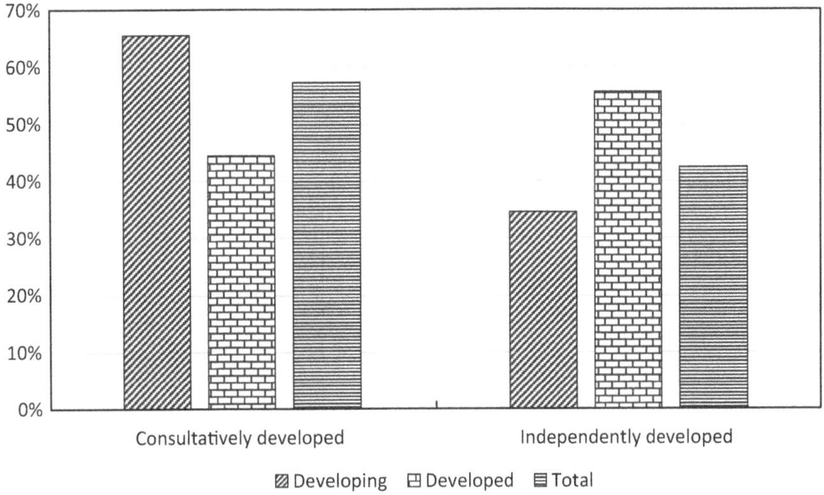

Figure 4.2 How are the audit criteria you use for environmental performance audits developed: (a) consultatively; and (b) independently? Response (percentage) – developing SAIs (N = 29); developed SAIs (N = 18); total SAIs (N = 47).

challenges in developing criteria for environmental programmes, developing SAIs find it helpful to consult auditees. Developed SAIs, possessing more resources and/or more expertise and experience in conducting performance audits may not consider it necessary to consult auditees to the same degree.

Explicit versus implicit audit criteria

The criteria for environmental performance audits are specified: (a) explicitly by a little more than two-thirds of SAIs; and (b) conveyed or understood implicitly by about one-third of SAIs. A larger proportion of developed SAIs (about four-fifths) than the developing SAIs (two-thirds) specify audit criteria explicitly. Consistent with expectations, this suggests more expertise and experience in developed SAIs compared with developing SAIs in undertaking environmental performance audit. However, in both groups, a large majority of SAIs specify audit criteria explicitly. This is notable, given that developing criteria for environmental performance audits in itself are considered challenging (INTOSAI, 2012); expressing them explicitly would be more so.

Many environmental problems display attributes including broad and variable temporal and spatial scales, complexity and uncertainty, multiple causes, lack of clear policy instruments, multiple disciplines and multiple stakeholders (APSC, 2007: 3–4; Dovers, 2005: 44–49). Consequently, many environmental policies and programmes have aspirational rather than concrete goals, such as optimizing

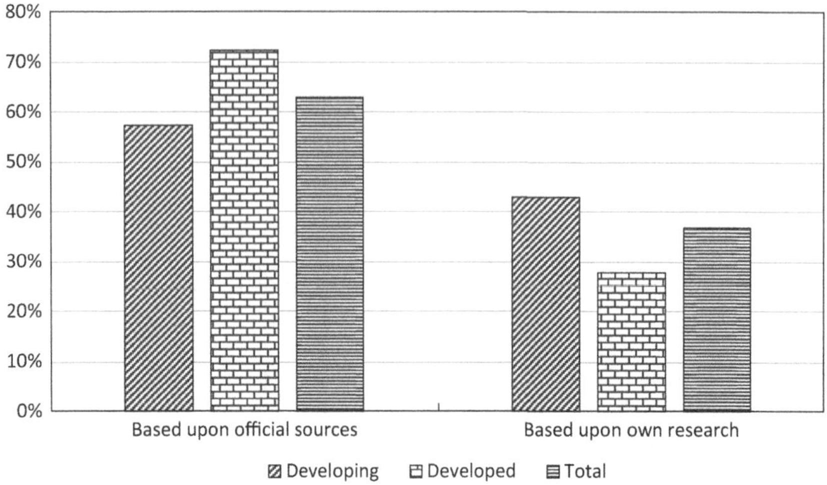

Figure 4.3 How are the audit criteria you use for environmental performance audits sourced: (a) official sources; or (b) own research? Response (percentage) – developing SAIs (N = 28); developed SAIs (N = 18); total SAIs (N = 46).

economic, social and environmental outcomes (e.g. Australia's federal *Water Act*, 2007). These goals sometimes may even be conflicting. In these circumstances, a large majority of both developed and developing SAIs being able to explicitly express audit criteria for environmental performance audits is considered to be an admirable achievement.

Source of audit criteria

About two-thirds of SAIs (Figure 4.3) derive the criteria for environmental performance audits from official sources (such as targets in legislation, policy and auditees' own plans), and about one-third develop them through their own research. This likely suggests that, while a majority of environmental policies and programmes may have sufficiently defined objectives to enable constructing audit criteria based upon them, a significantly large proportion (one-third) may have unclear or vague goals that could not be translated into audit criteria. Hence SAIs, in these cases, would have to develop criteria through their own research, such as, literature survey and international benchmarking.

Compared with developing SAIs (57 per cent), a higher proportion of developed SAIs (72 per cent) seem to be deriving the criteria for environmental performance audits from official sources. This likely suggests that, compared with developing countries, environmental policies and programmes in developed countries have more clearly defined objectives. This is consistent with expectations, as developed countries, being early leaders in the environmental policy domain and generally having a more accountable governance framework than developing countries, are likely to be more articulate in defining the objectives of their environmental policies and programmes than their developing peers.

Of the SAIs (about two-thirds in Figure 4.3) that use official sources (e.g. auditee's own performance indicators) for deriving audit criteria, only about half of them consider that they are adequate, realistic and/or fair (20 per cent specifically indicating in the negative). This suggests a high degree of scepticism about the reliability of official sources. This is not surprising, as public administration officials are known to have developed performance targets that will portray them in a good light (Pollitt, 2013). SAIs maintaining a sceptical view of public administration is not a bad thing in itself: in fact, this is the essence of public auditing. Public auditors' professional scepticism, their critical approach to the information provided and their objective distance from it, are considered vital for auditing (CAG, 2014: 15). In view of this, it is not surprising that SAIs, irrespective of their developmental status, have a fairly similar view of the matter. There is very little difference between the developing SAIs and developed SAIs on how they perceive the official sources of information.

SAIs observations on audit criteria

A majority of SAIs in their opinion indicate that 'audit criteria are based on a number of sources' that include both 'official guidance' 'if available' and their own 'research for best practice' in 'audit literature and standards', as well as 'standards set under international conventions'. The views of SAIs on this matter are succinctly captured in one SAI's observation:

> We always set criteria to determine the audit test required to answer audit questions. To the extent possible these criteria will be based on clear standards and agreed with the auditee. Sometimes the criteria are set in legislation or in management plans, but often not. Where there is a lack of official criteria, and we develop to some extent our own, we still validate these based on available international best practice, our experience with comparable audits, or expert advice. The lack of official criteria can already indicate a potential audit finding i.e. if the auditee cannot assess its own performance, it is unlikely to be effective or efficient. We always discuss audit criteria with the auditee as part of our audit planning.

Only a few SAIs indicate having full confidence in official criteria. One such SAI notes that 'they are adequate because we assume that their development is guided by the international standards and best practice where applicable'. Others that do not discount the value of official criteria, still express reservations about them, such as: (1) 'Most of the used criteria come from official documents but they can be too easy to reach (not ambitious enough). If they are so, we sometimes criticize the definition of their criteria'; (2) 'The auditees' criteria are not always adequate to measure performance. So, we critically examine them'; (3) 'Sometimes official criteria are realistic and measurable and sometimes [they are] not'; (4) 'The auditees own criteria are often biased or not relevant for answering the audit questions'; and (5) 'The indicators do not measure the level of implementation of the goals.' These comments are consistent with the high degree of scepticism in SAIs about official sources of criteria, as noted above.

Methods used for evidence collection

Methods for evidence collection used by SAIs in environmental performance auditing (Figure 4.4), in the order of their popularity, appear to be:

More frequently used (about 50 per cent and above):

1. document examination (96 per cent);
2. officials interview (85 per cent);
3. site visit (75 per cent),
4. literature survey (67 per cent);
5. system/process review (64 per cent);
6. sample examination (60 per cent),
7. expert opinion (48 per cent); and
8. stakeholders consultation (47 per cent).

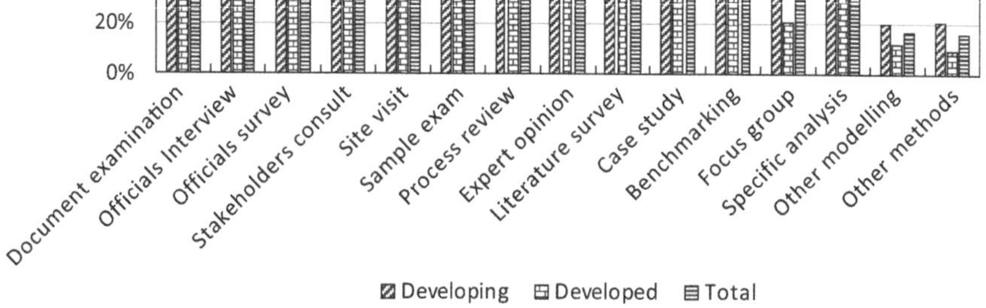

Figure 4.4 What methods did you use for evidence gathering in environmental performance audits in the last five years? Response (percentage) – developing SAIs (N = 29); developed SAIs (N = 18); total SAIs (N = 47) weighted as follows: (1) mostly/always (90 per cent or more of the time) – 1; (2) very often (50–89 per cent of the time) – 0.75; (3) often (30–49 per cent of the time) – 0.5; (4) occasionally (10–29 per cent of the time) – 0.25; and (5) rarely/never (less than 10 per cent of the time) – 0.10.

Less frequently used (below 50 per cent):

9. case study (44 per cent);
10. benchmarking (44 per cent);
11. officials survey (42 per cent);
12. specific economic/statistical analysis (41 per cent);
13. focus group (29 per cent);
14. other modelling (such as hydrological/ecological (17 per cent); and
15. other methods (16 per cent).

The data inspection shows that only document examination and officials interview could be considered as almost always used. A WGEA (2013: 52–54) study related to audit of water issues found that document examination was used 95 per cent of the time, and interview of officials was used 90 per cent of the time. Site visit, with 60 per cent use, came third in that study.

Except for the five less commonly used methods – officials survey; benchmarking; focus groups; other modelling; and one unspecified, other methods – the developed country SAIs seem to be using all methods more frequently than the developing SAIs. The largest difference in the use between developed and developing country SAIs is in relation to three methods: (1) literature survey (27 per cent); (2) officials interview (22 per cent); and (3) stakeholders consultation (22 per cent). Compared with developing SAIs, the higher use of literature survey (more time and resources required) and stakeholders' consultation (reflects more consultative governance) by the developed SAIs is consistent with expectations. However, the higher use of interview of officials by developed SAIs is not intuitive and needs explanation. The lower use of this method by developing SAIs is a better characterization of this issue. One explanation could be that, in addition to the document examination, the developing SAIs may be relying more upon indirect interactions such as officials survey and some other secondary information to make conclusions. It may be considered as an extension of a less consultative approach to performance auditing by developing SAIs than used by developed SAIs. There is some anecdotal evidence to this effect (McPhee, Former Auditor General of Australia, personal communication).

Another explanation could be that the developing SAIs' lower use of most methods is balanced by somewhat higher use of less frequently used methods such as officials survey, benchmarking and focus groups. The focus group seems to be 15 per cent more prominently used by developing SAIs than the developed SAIs. Difficulty in developing audit criteria (CAG, 2014: 28; McPhee, personal communication) – more so for environmental performance audits – could be encouraging developing SAIs to engage more in focus groups, to get the audit going, compared with the developed SAIs that may be more experienced in developing them. On the face of it, this appears to be more consultative. However, this may also suggest a lower degree of productive relationship between the SAIs and public administration officials in developing SAIs than in the developed SAIs. This is corroborated for one developing country SAI by the study described in Chapter 5.

The overall lesser use of most methods by the developing SAIs, however, is not completely balanced by the higher use of some less frequently used methods. The overall deficit of 60 per cent (or average of 4 per cent per method) is more than could be attributed to a sampling error. This seems to point to some systemic difference between the two groups of SAIs. Using a 50 per cent threshold as an approximation for a method being frequently used, it is observed that, on average, developed SAIs (eight) are using more methods than the developing SAIs (six). This is partly validated, as will be seen in Chapter 5. Using more methods consumes more resources. Therefore, developed SAIs generally having more resources are likely to use more methods.

Considerations in the decision of methods for evidence collection

SAIs consider various factors in deciding which methods to use for evidence collection. These include: (1) 'the complexity of the topic'; (2) 'objectives' and 'scope of the audit (economy/efficiency/effectiveness)'; (3) resources – 'budgetary constraints' and 'availability of staff' and 'in house and external experts'. To decide which methods to use, sometimes they also undertake some further analysis, such as 'problem-tree analysis, process mapping' and 'risk analysis that consider the likelihood of deviations and possible impact of such deviations' on the results to identify 'the weaker controls'. The following three observations of SAIs describe the essence of the method selection.

1 Audit methodology is highly dependent on the best sources of available information upon which to quickly gain an accurate understanding of the audit matter and provide a sound base for our audit findings, conclusions and recommendations.
2 Audit methodology is determined by the nature and extent of evidence required to enable us to conclude on our audit questions based on the audit criteria. We endeavor to obtain corroborative evidence from different sources. Any limitations on available evidence may also determine to some extent the audit question i.e. we may not attempt to answer a very general or highly technical question. Where we do not have expertise in-house to address an audit question, we will either procure the expertise; hire experts on a short term basis; use focus groups; or consult with recognized experts.
3 We mainly consider the methods we can apply by ourselves because in the times of the economic recession our financial resources to hire external experts were very limited. We always try to gather as many information as possible from auditees and also from different other relevant sources.

Standards and guidelines

Standards and guidelines are used in performance auditing for quality assurance. The highest proportion (88 per cent) of SAIs use international standards or equivalent guidelines for performance audit (Figure 4.5) in undertaking environmental

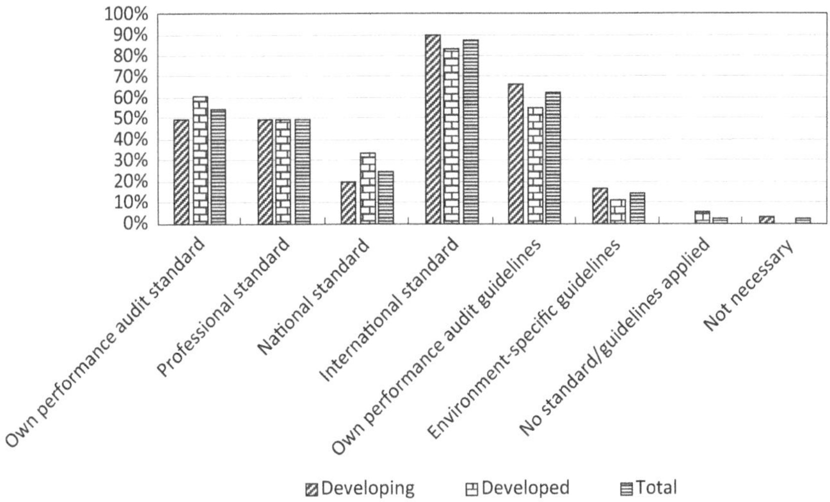

Figure 4.5 Do you use any standards or guidelines in conducting environmental performance audit? Multiple response (percentage) – developing SAIs (N = 30); developed SAIs (N = 18); total SAIs (N = 48).

performance audits, followed by their own performance audit guidelines (63 per cent); their own standards for performance audit (54 per cent); and professional standards for performance audit (50 per cent). About one-quarter of SAIs use their national standard for performance audit and a small proportion (15 per cent) use their own specific guidelines for environmental performance audit. Only 2 per cent of SAIs either do not use any standard or guideline or do not consider them necessary. It is noteworthy that the overwhelming majority of SAIs use some standard or guideline in undertaking environmental performance audits as a means of quality assurance. It is to be noted that percentages quoted here are not exclusive and hence not additive. SAIs were asked to select multiple standards and guidelines they use in environmental performance audits.

It is notable that a higher proportion of developing SAIs use: (a) international (INTOSAI, 2004) standards (90 per cent); (b) their own performance audit guideline (67 per cent); and (c) their own environment-specific guideline (17 per cent) for performance audit than their respective use by developed SAIs: (a) 83 per cent; (b) 56 per cent; and (c) 11 per cent. On the other hand, a higher proportion of developed SAIs use: (d) their own performance audit standard (61 per cent); and (e) national standards (33 per cent) compared with the respective use of these by developing SAIs: (d) 50 per cent; and (e) 20 per cent. It is noted that, compared with developed SAIs, a higher use of the former three standards or guidelines by the developing SAIs is almost balanced by their lower use of the latter two. It is considered that developing one's own standards or a national standard (highly likely that an SAI would play a key role there) requires more effort and hence resources than using the international (INTOSAI) standards, or developing and using one's own performance audit guidelines. This explains why more resourceful developed SAIs have a higher use of their own standard or national standard compared with the developing SAIs. However, considering that developing environment-specific guidelines for performance audit also requires effort and resources, a higher use of them by developing SAIs compared with developed SAIs is not intuitive and needs explanation. It is conceivable that such specific guidelines might either have been influenced by or developed in collaboration with WGEA and/or its Regional Groups. For example, ASOSAI, the majority of whose members comprise developing SAIs, has developed a specific *Guidance for Environmental Auditing* (ASOSAI, 2009). Due to the cost-effectiveness involved, developing SAIs are more likely to follow international leads on such matters than are developed SAIs. This seems to be a plausible explanation for higher use of environment-specific guidelines for performance auditing by developing SAIs than by developed SAIs.

A higher proportion of developed SAIs (6 per cent) than developing SAIs (0 per cent) do not use any standards or guidelines. On the other hand, a higher proportion (3 per cent) of developing SAIs than developed SAIs (0 per cent) consider that the use of standards or guidelines is not necessary. Both of these practices are similar. While the difference between the two groups of SAIs is statistically significant in each case, the percentages involved are very low. Due to these reasons, these practices are considered an exception rather than the norm.

Auditing of effectiveness

As noted in Chapter 2, the concept of effectiveness is a contentious matter in regard to whether it should refer to substantive/policy effectiveness (actual impact or outcome), or administrative effectiveness of systems and process (output versus input). Auditing the former is more challenging than the latter. Not surprisingly, only a small proportion SAIs (13 per cent) seem to audit the effectiveness of policy (Figure 4.6), and a slightly larger proportion (17 per cent) audit the adequacy of systems and processes. However, the fact that more than two-thirds of SAIs indicate they audit both the policy (substantive) and system/process (administrative) effectiveness may come as a surprise. The auditing of both substantive and administrative effectiveness by SAIs suggests that perhaps there is a disconnect between academics (e.g. Pollitt and Mul, 1999; Put, 2011) and practitioners on the matter – with the former stressing the 'purity' of concept and the latter taking a more pragmatic view.

Compared with the developed SAIs, about 10 per cent more developing country SAIs endeavour to audit the effectiveness of policy, and about 10 per cent fewer developing country SAIs endeavour to audit the effectiveness of system and processes (such as the use of key performance indicators). This is consistent with expectations, as compared with their developed peers the developing SAIs continue to have a higher focus directly on results rather than system and processes to achieve them. However, it is interesting to note that the difference between

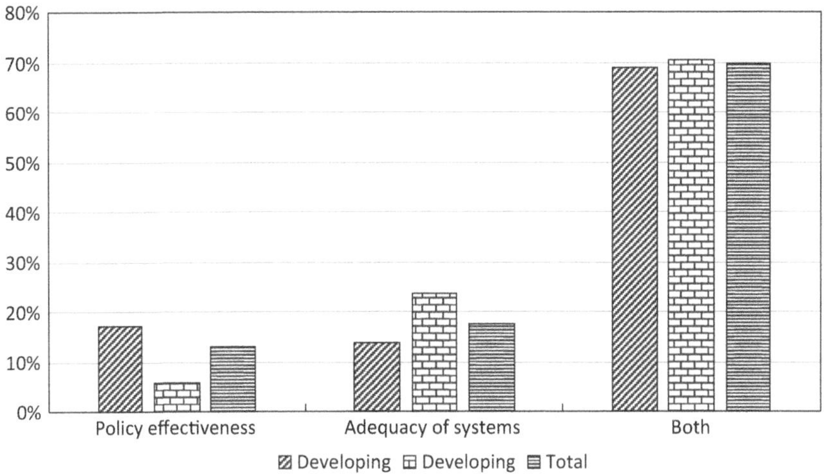

Figure 4.6 Whether or not auditees report on the effectiveness of the environmental policies and programmes they implement, do you assess: (a) policy effectiveness; (b) system and processes; (c) both (a) and (b)? Response (percentage) – developing SAIs (N = 29); developed SAIs (N = 17); total SAIs (N = 46).

the developing and developed SAIs ends there. Irrespective of their development status, more than two-thirds of both developing and developed SAIs indicate auditing both substantive and administrative effectiveness. As noted in the previous paragraph, this suggests that some conceptual differences between academics and practitioners exist on the notion of effectiveness. This could be interpreted as reasonable divergence between theory and practice.

Clearance process for performance audits

Receiving formal comments on draft performance audit reports and incorporating them into final reports is more than a benign process of auditees' feedback. As noted in Chapter 2, effectively it is a clearance process that may be contentious. An overwhelmingly large proportion (72 per cent) of SAIs seem to be either 'very satisfied' or 'satisfied' with the clearance process (Figure 4.7), whereas a significant proportion (28 per cent) seem to be 'neutral' – neither satisfied nor dissatisfied with the report clearance process. No SAI seem to be 'dissatisfied' or 'very dissatisfied'. This suggests a good engagement by SAIs with the auditees – a sign of a healthy professional relationship, perhaps in contrast with a traditional impression of distrust between auditors and auditees.

The SAIs response on the clearance process reflecting on their relationship with the auditees becomes clearer by the contrast between developing and developed SAIs. Compared with about 60 per cent of developing SAIs, close to

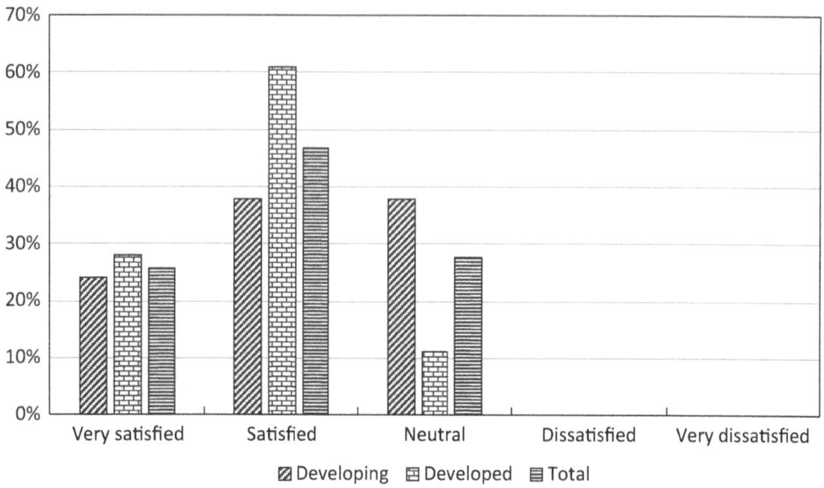

Figure 4.7 How satisfied you are with the clearance process for environmental performance audits with the auditees? Response (percentage) – developing SAIs (N = 29); developed SAIs (N = 18); total SAIs (N = 47).

90 per cent of developed SAIs seem to be either 'very satisfied' or 'satisfied' with the clearance process. More consultative and less adversarial relationships between SAIs and auditees is more likely in developed countries than in developing countries, possibility due to more familiarity and comfort with auditing as an accountability mechanism. There is anecdotal (McPhee, personal communication) as well as documented evidence (as noted in Chapter 5) to this effect.

SAIs' observation on the clearance process

Notwithstanding some challenges involved, a general satisfaction among SAIs on the clearance process for environmental performance audits is also evident from their observations. One SAI notes that 'the issues are not different from any [other] audit. Once the audited entity accepts that the audit was fair, objective and accepts the findings, they proceed to effect the recommendations'. Some SAIs indicate specific time frame for response, others observe that 'discussions with auditees take a long time'. While not dissimilar to other audits, challenges 'depend on problems and [auditees]'. 'The challenges may come when [some] auditees are not serious when the report is sent to them for comments and factual clearance and would want some of the audit findings and conclusions be modified or removed in the last minute.' Some SAIs indicate that due to their mandate they are not dependent on auditees' consent. One such SAI observes that while 'clearance is not an applicable concept', 'we strive to achieve a common understanding on the central elements of the audit (criteria, major findings etc.) in order for the audit to add maximum value'.

Cooperation among SAIs and contribution of the WGEA to environmental auditing

Four types of cooperation occurring among SAIs in order of popularity as per the five WGEA surveys during the period, 2003–2012. These are: (1) exchange of audit information or environmental auditing experiences; (2) audit of an international environmental accord; (3) environmental audit, other than of an agreement or treaty; and (4) cooperation on transboundary environmental issues. While the WGEA, through its surveys, has been tracking the growth of cooperation among SAIs, this study investigates how SAIs perceive various benefits derived from cooperation either directly or indirectly via the WGEA. In doing so, this study also evaluates the advantage of international cooperation among SAIs on auditing of international environmental agreements, as suggested by Van Leeuwen (2004), who first reported on the activities of the WGEA.

Benefits of cooperation generally

An overwhelmingly large proportion of SAIs (Figure 4.8) consider that cooperation with other SAIs, directly or indirectly via the WGEA or other INTOSAI groups, has benefited them in relation to:

1 improved understanding of environmental matters (94 per cent);
2 improved skill of staff (81 per cent); and
3 lifting the profile of environmental performance auditing generally (92 per cent).

On all aspects, a higher proportion of the developing SAIs than that of the developed SAIs perceive benefits of cooperation, noting, though, that a large majority of the developed SAIs also consider cooperation to be beneficial. The difference in perception of benefits between the developing and developed SAIs is largest in relation to the improvement in the skills of staff and smallest in relation to lifting the profile of environmental performance auditing generally. It is considered that, due to their already relatively better staff experience and expertise, it is likely that a lesser proportion of developed SAIs than of developing SAIs perceive cooperation as leading to the benefit of improvement in staff skills. This, however, does not diminish the fact that a very large majority of all SAIs consider cooperation beneficial on all aspects, including improvement in staff skills.

SAIs, in their observations, list several benefits of cooperation. These include the following: (1) 'Sharing of ideas, experiences, challenges and suggestions on how to [overcome] them'; (2) 'Exchange of methodologies and knowledge'; (3) 'Exchange of good practices'; (4) 'Training about environmental audit'; (5) '[T]he use of information from other SAIs and sample previous audits as a learning tool'; and (6) 'Capacity building, build[ing] a common approach, [and] follow up the implementation of international agreements'. The following two observations broadly capture the views of the SAIs on the matter:

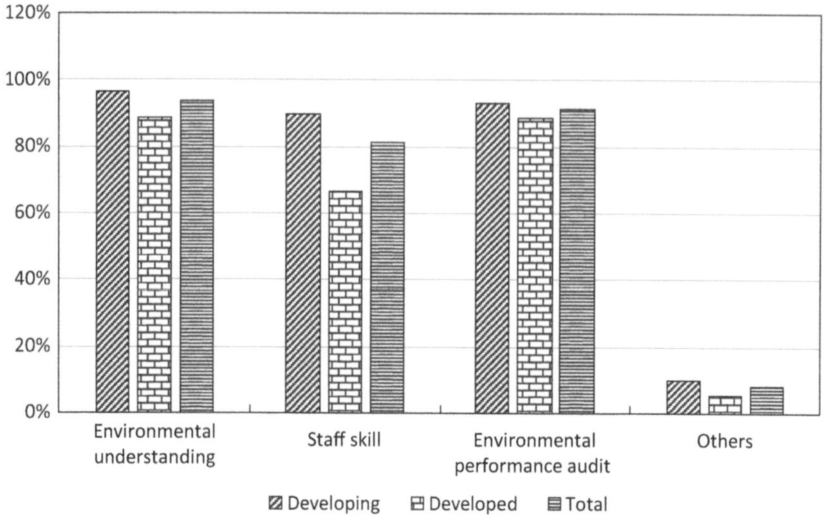

Figure 4.8 Has the cooperation with other SAIs either directly or indirectly via INTOSAI (Regional Group or WGEA) benefited your SAI by contributing to any benefits related to: (a) improved understanding of environmental matters; (b) improved skill of staff; (c) lifting the profile of environmental performance auditing generally; and (d) other matters? 'Yes' response (percentage) – developing SAIs (N = 30); developed SAIs (N = 18); total SAIs (N = 48) weighted as follows: (1) Yes – 1; and (2) No and N/A – 0.

1 The problems are often similar in different countries and discussions/cooperation with competent staff in other SAIs provides a valuable arena for learning. Other SAIs have often already done audits in areas we are planning to audit. This serves as valuable input in the design of our audits. Audits on environmental issues often has a transboundary scope (like air pollution, CO2 emissions and waste). Information gathering and cooperation with other SAIs are often crucial for the ability our SAI has to perform/finalize this type of audits.
2 The contacts with other SAI's facilitates our audit planning and we can share best practices, good ideas, and experiences. Seeing the different approaches taken by our international peers is a good learning opportunity. WGEA provides access to a good network of experts in environmental auditing, which is beneficial to our own audit approach.

Benefits of cooperation on the audit of the international environmental agreements

Nearly all SAIs (98 per cent) consider that compared with individual audits, cooperative audits of the implementation of the international environmental

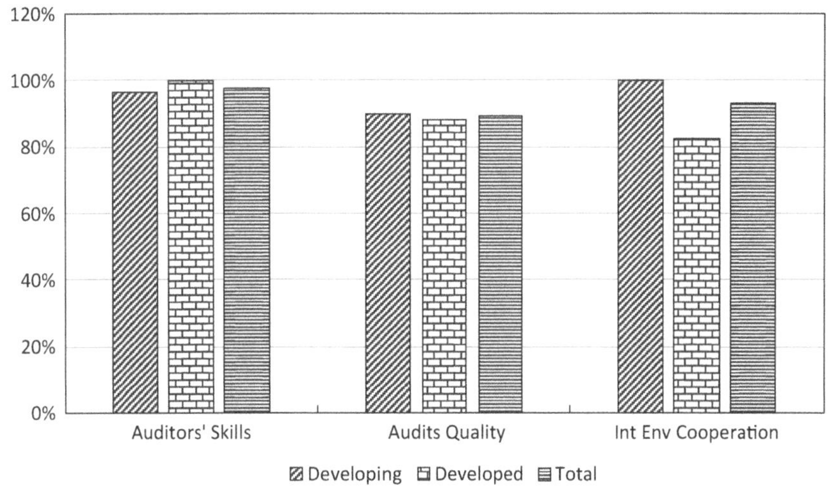

Figure 4.9 Do you consider that, compared with audit by a single SAI, joint/cooperative audits with other SAIs of the implementation of the international environmental agreements contribute more to: (a) the professional skills of the auditors; (b) the quality of the audits; and (c) international environmental cooperation? 'Yes' response (percentage) – developing SAIs (N = 29); developed SAIs (N = 17); total SAIs (N = 46) weighted as follows: (1) Yes – 1; and (2) No and N/A – 0.

agreements contribute more to the professional skills of the auditors (Figure 4.9). Overwhelming majorities of the SAIs also consider that compared with individual audits, cooperative audits contribute more to audit quality (89 per cent of SAIs); and international environmental cooperation (93 per cent). There is very little difference in the perception of developing and developed SAIs on the relative benefits of cooperative audits relating to 'auditors' skills' and 'audit quality'. However, about 20 per cent more developing SAIs than developed SAIs consider that cooperative audits contribute more to international environmental cooperation. The more positive assessment of this benefit by the developing SAIs may be because, compared with the developed SAIs, they perceive international cooperation more favourably, as they are perhaps net receivers of its benefits. Leaving aside some differences on some aspects of the benefits between the developing and developed SAIs, an overwhelming majority of all SAIs consider that, compared with individual audits, cooperative implementation of the international environmental agreements contribute more to audit skills, audit quality and international environmental cooperation.

Conclusions in the previous section and this section suggest that SAIs strongly consider that international cooperation is beneficial to them. This is a strong endorsement of the WGEA work by SAIs. It reinforces the conclusion reached in Chapter 3 that the WGEA has a very positive influence on the development of environmental auditing. Almost all SAIs that chose to comment (44 per cent) on the matter were very positive. The following three observations broadly summarize their views:

1 Joint/Cooperative audits assist SAIs to share methodologies on how to conduct different audits and share issues to consider most in different audits and for SAIs which have not yet conducted audits on certain areas to learn lessons from those which have already conducted them.
2 Cooperative audits enhance communication on the audit and provide the opportunity for capacity building of auditors.
3 Conducting parallel audits and discussion of joint reports on the same topic improve the quality of the audit and provide an integrated approach.

Conclusion

Environment matters have entered the mainstream of performance auditing at least in the strategic sense. SAIs predominantly select environmental topics for performance auditing using a risk-based structured approach. Performance audit criteria are generally developed in consultation with auditees. Economic factors influence the choice of methods, with developed country SAIs using more resource-intensive methods than their developing peers. Compared with developing country SAIs, developed country SAIs generally use more system-oriented approaches and are more consultative. The high prevalence of auditing of both substantive and administrative effectiveness by SAIs suggests that perhaps there is a disconnect between academics' and practitioners' views on the matter. Almost all SAIs use some standards or guidelines for quality assurance of their environmental performance audit. SAIs overwhelmingly consider that cooperation with other SAIs has benefited them.

Having studied environmental performance auditing at a global (macro) scale in Chapters 3 and 4, the next chapter will have a closer look (microscopic) at the phenomena by a comparative study of environmental performance auditing in three countries – Australia, Canada and India.

Note

1 The original target participant group for the survey was made up of the 103 SAIs (72 developing and 31 developed countries). These SAIs were identified as having some experience in undertaking environmental performance audits during the two-decade period 1992–2012 based upon the analysis reported in Chapter 3. The WGEA, however, sent the survey to about 200 SAIs on its contact list. Only four SAIs outside the original target group responded, demonstrating their experience in conducting environmental performance audits. This not only validated the criteria for forming the target group, but also extended the conclusion (earlier reached in Chapter 3) to 2016 that about 50 per cent of SAIs are not contributing to the global corpus of environmental performance audits.

References

APSC. (2007). *Tackling Wicked Problems: A Public Policy Perspective*. Canberra: Australian Public Service Commission.

ASOSAI. (2009). *Guidance on Conducting Environmental Audit*. ASOSAI.

CAG. (2014). *Performance Auditing Guidelines, 2014*. New Delhi: Comptroller and Auditor General of India.

Dovers, S. (2005). *Environment and Sustainability Policy: Creation, Implementation, Evaluation*. Leichardt: Federation Press.

INTOSAI. (2004). *Performance Audit Guidelines: ISSAI 3000–3100*. Stockholm: INTOSAI.

INTOSAI. (2012). Environmental auditing: current and future challenges. *International Journal of Government Auditing*, 39(3), 21–22.

Pollitt, C. (2013). The logics of performance management. *Evaluation*, 19(4), 346–363.

Pollitt, C. & Mul, R. (1999). Criteria. In C. Pollitt, X. Girre, J. Lonsdale, R. Mul, H. Summa & M. Waerness (Eds), *Performance or Compliance* (pp. 79–104). Oxford: Oxford University Press.

Pollitt, C. & Summa, H. (1997). Reflexive watchdogs? How supreme audit institutions account for themselves. *Public Administration*, 75(2), 313–336.

Put, V. (2011). Norms used: some strategic considerations from the Netherlands and the UK. In J. Lonsdale, P. Wilkins & T. Ling (Eds), *Performance Auditing: Contributing to Accountability in Democratic Government* (pp. 75–94). Cheltenham: Edward Elgar.

Rika, N. (2009). What motivates environmental auditing? A public sector perspective. *Pacific Accounting Review*, 21(3), 304–318. doi: 10.1108/01140580911012520

Van Leeuwen, S. (2004). Developments in environmental auditing by supreme audit institutions. *Environmental Management*, 33(2), 163–172.

WGEA. (2012). Work plans. Retrieved 27 February 2016 from http://environmental-auditing.org/Home/WGEAActivities/WorkPlans/tabid/112/Default.aspx.

WGEA. (2013). *Auditing Water Issues: An Examination of SAIs' Experiences and the Methodological Tools They Have Successfully Used*. Stockholm: INTOSAI.

5 Environmental performance auditing in three countries

The earlier chapters, by describing the basic relevant concepts, global trends and global practices, have provided the bigger or macroscopic picture of the discipline of environmental performance auditing. This chapter, by investigating concrete examples of environmental performance auditing in three countries – Australia, Canada and India – presents a detailed or microscopic view of the practice of environmental performance auditing. This study is not about auditing in the three countries *per se*, but is used as a means of exploring the practice of environmental performance auditing in more detail. Australia, Canada and India present good examples for this purpose for two reasons. First, together they possess significant similarity and diversity. In terms of similarity, all three are federations with Westminster-type parliamentary democracies, and their Supreme Audit Institutions (SAIs) are independent. In terms of diversity, Australia and Canada are developed countries, while India is still a developing country. Further, the Australian and Indian SAIs do not have specific powers for auditing environmental matters, while the Canadian SAI does have such powers. Second, all three have been significantly active in environmental performance auditing. Over the two decades 1992–2012, in terms of output of environmental performance audits globally, Australia (38 audits) ranked nineteenth; Canada (135 audits) second; and India (24 audits) ranked thirty-first (Prasad, 2016: 208).

A brief introduction of mandate and institutional arrangements of SAIs of the three countries is presented for context. Subsequently, the environmental performance audit planning and control framework of the three countries are described. Their current practice is investigated through a content analysis of five years of environmental performance audit reports (Australia, 22; Canada, 30; and India, 20; total, 72) for the period, 2010–2014 (a five-year period comparable to current practice investigation in Chapter 4). The observations from the content analysis of audit reports present 'what is'. This is compared with the relevant requirements of SAIs' standards, manuals and guidelines presenting 'what should be' in terms of audit speak to draw some conclusions about their practice.

Mandate and institutional arrangements

The SAI of Australia (the Auditor General together with the office that supports it) is called the Australian National Audit Office (ANAO). The SAI of Canada together with its office is called Office of the Auditor Genera (OAG). The SAI of India together with its supporting Department of Audit and Account is called the Comptroller and Auditor General (CAG). Each of the three SAIs is more than a century old. Having a common British heritage, the Australian, Canadian and Indian SAIs are similar in most respects. They are independent statutory institutions, not subject to any direction in selection of topics of performance audits and methods employed to audit them; and have full power to call witnesses and documents. They report their findings to parliament and assist it via public account committee or other relevant committees to hold the executive government to account. The three SAIs undertake financial, compliance and performance audits. The CAG also prepares the accounts of the central and state (provincial) governments and maintains the superannuation accounts of their employees (public servants). Notwithstanding similarities, there are some notable and subtle differences in jurisdiction, independence and reporting arrangements.

Jurisdiction

The Indian SAI's jurisdiction includes all three levels of government – federal, state (provincial) and local. However, with some exceptions, the Australian and Canadian (includes three territories – Nunavut, the Yukon and the Northwest Territories) SAIs have jurisdiction only over the federal government. Further, unlike its Australian and Indian peers, the Canadian SAI has a specific mandate to audit environmental matters. The Commissioner of the Environment and Sustainable Development (CESD), a statutory official within the Canadian SAI with a dedicated workforce, undertakes this function and reports directly to parliament. Under the Canadian *Auditor General Act*, 1995 the CESD:

- conducts performance audits and studies to monitor the federal government's management of environmental and sustainable development issues;
- monitors the quality, fairness and implementation of sustainable development strategies of federal departments; and
- administers the statutory environmental petitions process through which Canadians can ask the federal government to respond to their concerns about the environment and sustainable development (OAG, 2014g).

The CESD is considered a model institution that could be usefully examined by other countries (OECD, 2004: 2; Rose, 2001). An independent review by the Green Ribbon Panel (Dowdeswell et al., 2007: 9) concluded that 'the OAG and Commissioner have had a positive impact on the federal government's management of environmental and sustainable development issues. They have developed a strong domestic and international reputation as a centre of excellence in environmental auditing.'

It is interesting to note that Canada produces only about 30 performance audits compared to Australia's 50 performance audits per annum (Wilson, 2011: 32). However, Canada's environmental performance auditing output is three to four times that of Australia (for the period 1992–2012, 3.5 times and for the period 2003–2012, 3 times higher). Given the economic similarity between them, the higher output of environmental performance audits as a proportion of total performance audits in Canada could reasonably be attributed to the OAG's specific mandate on environmental auditing and consequent dedicated resources and focus. This indicates that a specific audit mandate can, and does, make a difference, notwithstanding the WGEA observation (see, for example, WGEA, 2004: ii; 2007: 23; 2012: 11) that the absence of a specific mandate is not a barrier to environmental auditing.

Independence

The Indian SAI's independence is considered more secure than its Australian and Canadian peers, because its financial independence from political negotiation in parliament. The Indian SAI's expenses are directly charged to the consolidated fund of India. As it does not have to negotiate its budget with the executive and its budget is not subject to parliamentary approval, it is not exposed to any direct or indirect pressure. Unlike their Indian counterpart, both the Australian and Canadian SAIs' budgets are negotiated with the executive and are subject to parliamentary appropriation. This creates some dependence on the executive, and hence, in theory, has the potential to compromise the independence of the Australian and Canadian SAIs. Compromise or potential compromise of independence due to the dependence on the executive for budget is a valid concern that has been raised by no less than an Auditor General (McGlashan, 2014: 7–8). The Canadian and Australian SAIs' budgets are reviewed and recommended by a committee of their parliament. Both of these arrangements minimize the likelihood of any interference in the working of the Australian and Canadian SAIs. However, they do not eliminate the possibility of indirect pressure on the SAIs through budgetary means; given that under the Westminster model in both countries, the majority party (or group of parties) in the lower house that controls the budget also runs the government (executive). So there remains a possibility, however miniscule it may be, that a government (executive or majority party) in Australia or Canada not comfortable with the audit findings may apply undue pressure on SAIs through budgetary means, thus compromising their independence.

Institutional arrangements

The institutional arrangements of the three SAIs reflects their mandate. With a few exceptions, the institutional arrangements of the SAIs of Australia and Canada are similar. The Australian (one office, 350 staff) and Canadian (five offices, 600 staff) SAIs have very few offices and moderate staff strength. On the other hand, the Indian SAI is a very large organization with 48,000 staff (CAG, 2014b: iii, 78) in 141 offices, including in some overseas posts (Australia et al., 2012: 16). The large number of CAG staff needs to be seen in the context of its wide mandate over: (1) the departments and associated bodies of the central government; (2) 36 states and territory governments; and (3) thousands of local governments.

The ANAO has internal units with performance audit responsibilities for different portfolios or a group of government departments/portfolios. One such unit is responsible for auditing the matters related to the environment (Wilson, 2011: 25). In Canada, CESD, with about 40 people (Dowdeswell et al., 2007: 16), undertakes performance audit of the environment and sustainability-related issues. The CAG has established a nodal office for environmental audits. This office undertakes performance and compliance audits of the central (federal) government environmental programmes all over India. Additionally, the different state Accountant General offices also undertake performance and compliance audits of state-level environmental programmes (CAG, 2013d).

Submission of audit reports

While the ANAO and the OAG (and CESD) submit their reports directly to the legislature, the CAG submits its reports to the head of state (the President of India in the case of the central government and the relevant governor in the case of a state government) for laying before the relevant legislature. This is effectively reporting to the legislature via the executive. The current legislation does not prescribe any time limit within which a government should table the CAG report before the legislature. Legislative changes have been proposed for timely disclosure of the CAG report to the legislature (Australia et al., 2012: 17). As of December 2017, these changes were yet to materialize.

Performance audit planning

There are three types of planning for performance audits: (1) long-term (3–5 years) or strategic planning; (2) short-term annual planning for audit work; and (3) operational planning for individual audits. The first two are concerned with 'what to audit' and hence are related to the broader governmental work outside the SAIs' offices. This is the core of audit planning that is guided by their overall corporate strategic plans (e.g. vision, mission, objectives) or statements (ANAO, 2015a: 56) that they develop to steer their organization (CAG, 2014a: 19; OAG, 2014a;). The third issue is about 'how to audit' and mostly relates to the work inside the SAI offices. This is covered by SAIs' operational manuals and quality management framework (QMF).

Due to the wide range of government activities and limited audit resources, it is not possible to audit every aspect of government activity. The three SAIs have full discretion in choosing topics for performance audits. However, they necessarily need a process to determine what to audit. Broadly they all employ a similar 'risk-based approach' to choosing topics (ANAO, 2015a: 53; CAG, 2014a: 21–22; OAG, 2004: 21). They continuously scan government activities including through monitoring media reports, debate in parliament and its committees, portfolio/entity budget statements and entities' annual reports. Based upon this, they choose activities that pose the most significant risks; have greater potential to improve performance; and are of sufficient interest to public and parliament (see, for example, ANAO, 2015a: 54–55; OAG, 2014b). However, due to their different processes, as they have slightly different ways of selecting topics, it is worthwhile exploring these processes. The annual audit topic selection process in Australia is known as 'Blue Book' preparation; in Canada as 'One Pass Planning' (OPP); and in India as the 'Annual Audit Plan'.

Australia (Blue Book)

The ANAO's 'Blue Book' describes its annual audit coverage. It is a rolling annual programme of potential performance audits by portfolio that is updated every year. It is the product of a strategic and integrated approach to audit planning that is rigorous and consultative (Wilson, 2011: 29–31). The ANAO maintains an up-to-date knowledge base of the Australian government entities' operations on an ongoing basis and it periodically (annually) conducts an 'environmental scan' (a systematic way of data collection and analysis of factors that impact an organization) to identify key issues and challenges faced by the Australian public sector administration. With this information, the ANAO annually at its strategic planning session(s) first identifies potential audit issues for each portfolio. It then consolidates them and determines audits of significance by filtering the potential audit topics through considerations such as materiality, significance, potential impact and benefit, public/parliamentary interest, coverage (if covered by any recent audit or other studies or need for follow-up audit) and the ANAO's resource availability (ANAO, 2015a: 52–59). As it is mandatory for the ANAO to have regard to the audit priorities of the parliament, it provides the list of draft audit topics to the parliament's Joint Committee on Public Accounts and Audit (JCPAA that is equivalent of the generic public accounts committee, or PAC). It also simultaneously provides the draft list to government entities and other stakeholders for their comment. Following this, the planned audit work programme for the forthcoming year (the 'Blue Book') is finalized; its copies are provided to parliamentarians including the JCPAA and government entities; and it is also published on the ANAO website (ANAO, 2015a: 52–59; Wilson, 2011: 29).

Sometimes the ANAO undertakes performance audits that are not included in its annual audit work programme (Blue Book). These audits result from requests to the Auditor General from parliament, government or other parties. The Auditor General applies his or her discretion and considers each request on its own merit. An independent performance audit of ANAO has concluded that planning and scoping of the ANAO's annual audit work programme is efficient and effective (Wilson, 2011: 15).

Canada (One Pass Planning)

The OPP provide a systematic, integrated and risk-based approach to long-term audit planning (OAG, 2004: 21). Using knowledge regarding the business of government entities (updated periodically) and periodic environmental scanning, the OAG units, through OPP and other risk-based analyses, identify performance audit topics throughout the year. However, more intensive OPP for an entity is done every 5–6 years in consultation with government entities. On completion of OPPs for entities and functional areas, the OAG consolidates them each spring into a strategic audit plan (SAP) for five years. Being a long-term plan for audits of a sector or entity, the SAP is re-evaluated each year to ensure the right audits are planned (OAG, 2014b). Thus, the output of the OPP process is a SAP that identifies performance audits to be undertaken over the long-term (five years). A peer review recommends that the OAG give greater emphasis to the risk assessment phase of the audit planning process, to which the OAG has agreed (Australia et al., 2010: 13).

The performance audit planning processes in Australia 'and Canada are closely aligned' (Wilson, 2011: 33). As in Australia, an audit may be undertaken in response to a request from the government or a parliamentary committee.

India (Audit planning and the Audit Advisory Board)

Annual audit planning in India is undertaken by the field offices with reference to the CAG's strategic plans (CAG, 2014a: 19) that are at two levels:

- Long-term: the Strategic Plan outlines CAG's vision, mission and core values; the emerging issues for governance in India; organizational goals; and implementation arrangements (Australia et al., 2012: 23).
- Medium-term (five-year): the Perspective Plan focuses on medium- to long-term goals and challenges, and assigns responsibilities and identifies timelines for completion of specific tasks (Australia et al., 2012: 23).

The audits proposed in annual audit plans are typically based upon government entity profiles, financial materiality and risks, and also take into consideration the staff resources available (Australia et al., 2012: 13). The annual audit plans of field offices are reviewed by the CAG management considering the overall audit priorities, available resources and expectations across various offices. The approved audit plans are consolidated into the CAG's annual audit plan (CAG, 2014b: 10).

The CAG has established an Audit Advisory Board(s) for its head office in New Delhi and for each of its state audit offices. These boards comprise eminent persons and highly qualified professionals from diverse fields. The central Audit Advisory Board is chaired by the CAG personally, whereas the state Audit Advisory Boards are chaired by the respective state Accountants General. The purpose of the Audit Advisory Board(s) is to advise the CAG (and its state offices) on matters relating to audit (including audit topics) and suggest improvements in the performance and focus of audit (CAG, 2014b: 91–92). It reflects the CAG's openness to external advice, and is considered a 'good practice' (Australia et al., 2012: 24).

Overall, the audit planning of the ANAO is the most transparent of the three SAIs. Not only is its planning widely consultative, including with the public, its annual audit plans are also publicly available. On the other hand, not only is the audit planning of the OAG and CAG (notwithstanding CAG's audit advisory boards) less consultative, their audit plans are also not publicly available.

Good practices in performance audit planning and guidance

Notwithstanding their differences, the three SAIs exhibit some good practices in planning and undertaking performance audits. For example, ANAO publishes its 'Blue Book' (the finalized annual audit work programme) on its website, informing all interested parties – including the public – and it provides them an opportunity to make a contribution to every performance audit (ANAO, 2016a). The Canadian SAI has developed a manual, '4th E Practice Guide' to integrate environmental considerations in all its performance audit work (OAG, 2011b). And the Indian SAI has developed a separate 'Environment and Climate Change – Auditing Guidelines' (CAG, 2010a) to enable more effective environment audits.

Performance audit quality management framework: audit standards, manuals and guidelines

Variously named, the three SAIs have their own performance audit QMFs that comprise audit standards, policy manuals and/or guidelines. For example, OAG (2004: 10) calls it a quality management framework, whereas CAG (2014c: 1) calls it the Audit Quality Management Framework. The QMF is used here in a generic sense to denote a suite of documents (whether mandatory or voluntary) that are followed by the three SAIs to assure that their performance audits have been conducted in accordance with applicable laws, policies and professional standards. The key QMF documents used by the three SAIs to guide their performance audits are shown in Table 5.1.

Among a very few audit offices globally, the ANAO and OAG have adopted international auditing standards for their performance audit activities (Wilson, 2011: 32). The ANAO has adopted the standards (e.g. ASAE 3500) developed by the Australian Auditing and Assurance Standards Board (AUASB). ASAE 3500 (AUASB, 2008), however, seems to have been intentionally written for organizations other than audit offices, including, for example, internal auditors and private consultants that are not necessarily independent (Wilkins and Boyle, 2011). The ANAO conducts all its performance audits fully in accordance with its (AUASB) auditing standards (see, for example, ANAO, 2010a: 36; 2010b: 55). Similarly, the OAG follows the Chartered Professional Accountants (CPA) of Canada standards in its performance audit. However, unlike the ANAO, the OAG uses the CPA standards as the minimum requirements and also 'draws upon the standards and practices of other disciplines' (see, for example, OAG, 2010a: 29; 2010b: 30).

The Indian auditing standards (CAG, 2017) are largely based upon the International Organization of Supreme Audit Institutions Standards (INTOSAI, 2004) and are non-mandatory guidelines. Accordingly, the Indian auditing

Table 5.1 Quality management framework documents

QMF document	*Australia (ANAO)*	*Canada (OAG)*	*India (CAG)*
Standard	Australian Standard of Assurance Engagements (ASAE) – Performance Engagements – ASAE 3500, 2008 (ASAE 3000 also applies generally)	Chartered Professional Accountants (CPA) Canada Standard for Assurance Engagements, CPA Canada 5030	CAG's Auditing Standards, 2017
QMF		Performance Audit Quality Management Framework, 2004	Audit Quality Management Framework, 2014
Manual	Performance Audit Manual, 2015	Performance Audit Manual, 2014 (online)	Performance Audit Guideline, 2014 Environment and Climate Change Auditing Guidelines
Other materials	–	4th E Practice Guide	Practice guides on specific topics, e.g. planning individual performance audit

standards are mostly non-prescriptive. Unlike their Australian and Canadian counterparts, the Indian auditing standards enunciate principles rather than prescribe obligations. The Indian standards' non-prescriptive nature is highlighted by its preface, wherein trust is placed in audit officials to abide by them (CAG, 2017), rather than obliging them to do so.

In addition to containing the necessary information on their performance audits (e.g. mandate), and guiding instructions on their internal processes, the Australian and Canadian performance audit manuals embed the relevant provisions of their respective auditing standards. They clearly specify obligations required by standards or otherwise as 'shall' or 'should' policy statements (see, for example, ANAO, 2015a: 100–101; OAG, 2014c; 2014d). On the other hand, the Indian Performance Audit Guidelines (CAG, 2014a) state a broad range of principles and practices to be followed, leaving scope to improve their clarity, including by differentiating between obligations and matters of sound practice (Australia et al., 2012: 22). While CAG has updated its guidelines in 2014, this observation of the peer review (Australia et al., 2012) still remains valid.

There are five elements of the Canadian Performance Audit Quality Management Framework: leadership and planning, audit management, client focus, people management and continuous improvement (OAG, 2004: 116).

The Canadian Performance Audit Manual is designed to implement the OAG's 'Quality Management Framework' (OAG, 2004: 7). A peer review of the OAG (Australia et al., 2010: 1) concluded that except for minor improvements required to its risk assessment procedures and audit documentation, the OAG's quality management system was suitably designed to provide reasonable assurance about compliance with relevant legislative requirements and professional standards. Further, the system was operating effectively. The peer review identified several good practices of the OAG that might be of interest to other audit offices. These include: management of relationships with parliament; delivery of a clear message by its performance audit reports; its collaboration with other accountability offices; and development of criteria for performance audit of public corporations (Australia et al., 2010: 17).

Like the OAG's (2004: 118) framework, the CAG's Audit Quality Management Framework (AQMF) has five elements: leadership and direction, human resources management, audit management, clients and stakeholder relations and continuous improvement (CAG, 2014c: 2). The elements of this framework are mapped to the key instruments the CAG employs under each element, such as the Auditing Standards and the Performance Auditing Guidelines. The CAG has updated its AQMF based upon recommendations of the peer review (Australia et al., 2012: 21). However, a key enabler Performance Auditing Guidelines (updated but retains its earlier principles-based character) remains largely in its old form. As such, it appears it will be challenging for CAG to fully implement the intent of its AQMF in the short term.

On the more positive side, the CAG conducts internal peer review of its audit offices and inspects all field offices in a three-year cycle. Further, the CAG has a large network of 15 training centres (CAG, 2014b: 112–113) to train audit officials in the art and craft of audit. This network includes two international training centres: (1) the International Centre for Environment Audit and Sustainable Development (iCED); and (2) the International Centre for Information Systems and Audit. The iCED is a global training facility of the INTOSAI (CAG, 2014b: 84). During 2013–2014, the CAG training centres ran about 750 courses and trained about 13,000 audit officials in different aspects of audit (CAG, 2014b: 81). The CAG has taken several other measures aimed at quality improvement of performance audits. These include: (1) creation of a technical board of professional practice to consider policy issues related to auditing and accounting; and (2) issuance of guidance notes on interaction with auditees, and confidentiality of draft audit reports (CAG, 2014b: 73–74).

Reporting standards

The audit report is a critical component of performance audit. To some extent, it delivers functions that in other types of audits are provided by general standards of audit documentation (CAG, 2014a: 17). Being the end product of performance audits, the audit reports are what the parliament, public and media see of the work of Auditors General (OAG, 2004: 75). As the reputation and credibility of audit offices depend to a large extent on the quality of their reports, SAIs generally are very conscious of the content and presentation of their reports. Consequently, SAIs tend to specify them in their standards and/or manuals of practice. The Australian and Canadian reporting standards are obligations-based and hence prescriptive. On the other hand, the Indian standards only provide the framework for reporting in terms of general principles that an audit report should be complete, accurate, objective and convincing, noting that reporting may vary (CAG, 2017: 38). The non-obligatory nature of the Indian standards[1] (including for reporting) leave Indian auditors with greater discretion. This coupled with variable review of audit reports (Australia et al., 2012; 38) has potential to cause more variability in the quality of audit reports.

Current practice in environmental performance auditing

Audit objectives

All three SAIs require that objectives should be defined in a way that enables a conclusion against each of them. However, the OAG (2004: 27, 49) views on objectives are more stringent and better conform to a traditional view of audit ('what is' compared to 'what should be'). The key observations from the content analysis on the environmental performance audit objectives (Table 5.2) show that all Australian and Canadian environmental performance audit reports included audit objectives, whereas only 70 per cent of the Indian environmental performance audit reports did so. While this does not suggest that some Indian environmental performance audits did not have any audit objectives, it does indicate that many Indian audit reports (6 out of 20; 30 per cent) did not mention audit objectives. Noting that the inclusion of objectives in performance audit reports is mandatory, as per the then Indian standards (CAG, 2002) for reporting, it comes as a surprise that this proportion of Indian performance audit reports would not include audit objectives. On average, however, the Indian environmental performance audits had higher number (3.5) of objectives than the Australian (1.5) and Canadian (1.1) audits (Table 5.2). If the audit reports that did not quote audit objectives are excluded, the number of objectives per Indian performance audit becomes 4.9.

The objectives are the focus of the audit. The fewer the number of objectives, the more focused the performance audit is. The objectives analysis data in Table 5.2 suggest that the Australian and Canadian environmental performance audits are more focused than the Indian performance audits and the Canadian environmental performance audits are more focused than the Australian environmental performance audits. Not only did the Indian environmental performance audits, on average, have a higher number of objectives per audit, they also varied widely in terms of objectives. The minimum was zero (when audits with zero objectives are excluded, the minimum was three) and the maximum number of objectives in an Indian performance audit was eight. This is too many

Table 5.2 Audit objectives, approaches and criteria in environmental performance audit reports

Matter	*Australia*	*Canada*	*India*
Number of environmental audit reports (N)	22	28	20
A: Objectives			
Percentage of environmental performance reports quoting objectives	100	100	70
Minimum number of objectives in a performance audit	1	1	0
Maximum number of objectives in a performance audit	3	3	8
Average (mean) number of objectives per performance audit	1.5	1.1	3.5
Standard deviation (SD) of objectives	0.6	0.4	2.7
Coefficient of variation of objectives (SD/mean)	0.4	0.4	0.8
No of sub-objectives or line of inquiry per objective	2.6	1.6	1.0
B: Audit approaches			
System (percentage of performance audits)	91	79	45
Result (percentage of performance audits)	0	3	25
System and result (percentage of performance audits)	9	18	30
C: Criteria			
Percentage of performance audits quoting audit criteria	27	100	0
Percentage of performance audits explicitly quoting source(s) of audit criteria	0	100	100
Percentage of performance audits quoting explicit criteria	0	100	0
Criteria per objective/sub-objective	2.6	3.2	–

objectives to be addressed even from the recommended Indian practice, as the Indian performance auditing guidelines (CAG, 2014a: 27) recommends an upper limit of 3–5 for audit objectives. The presence of a large number of objectives in Indian performance audits has also been noted by an international peer review (Australia et al., 2012: 28) of the CAG. As each objective needs a conclusion, having too many objectives is likely to make conclusions challenging. This is likely to result in gaps between objectives and conclusions. The tightness of fit or alignment between the audit objectives and conclusions of an audit reflects the degree of rigour observed during an audit.

The coefficient of variation of audit objectives (Table 5.2) for India (0.8) is double that of Australia and Canada (both 0.4). This suggest that the number of objectives in Indian environmental performance audits are likely to vary twice as much as in Australian and Canadian audits. A statistical analysis of the objectives data suggests that the objectives of the Australian and Canadian performance audits were concentrated in two classes: (1–2) and (3–4). The maximum proportion (about 95 per cent or more) of the Australian and Canadian performance audits had 1–2 objectives and about 5 per cent or less had 3–4 (three as a maximum) objectives. On the other hand, the objectives of the Indian performance audits were spread over three classes: 3–4 (35 per cent): 5–6 (20 per cent); and 7–8 (15 per cent), if the 30 per cent of audits quoting no objectives are ignored. The spread of Indian performance audit objectives over several classes suggest differential treatment of audit objectives by diverse regional audit groups undertaking those audits. On the other hand, the Australian and Canadian environmental performance audits are undertaken by relatively less diverse groups. Consequently, the Australian and Canadian environmental performance audits demonstrate more consistency in terms of objectives.

There is considerable difference in number of sub-objectives per objective across the three SAIs (last row under objectives subheading in Table 5.2). However, this difference needs to be put in context. It is to be noted that the three SAIs treat sub-objectives differently. The CAG does not subdivide performance audits objectives into sub-objectives, so the matter rests here for India. However, the ANAO sometimes (about one in four audits) treats sub-objectives synonymously with audit criteria. The Australian figure of 2.6 has been derived using this approach. If only sub-objectives are considered, the figure becomes 1.9. The higher figure for Australian sub-objectives per objective (1.9 or 2.6) compared with the Canadian figure (1.6) indicates more refinement of audit objectives in the second stage. As discussed earlier, in the first stage the Canadian performance audit objectives (1.1 per audit) are already more sharply defined than the Australian audit objectives (1.5 per audit). Therefore, the higher refinement of Australian audit objectives in the second stage is consistent with expectations. A large number of objectives and no sub-objectives in Indian performance audits suggest scope for improvement in their focus.

In terms of the types of objectives, the most dominant objective type (more than 80 per cent) was the performance of government environmental policies and programmes followed by compliance with environmental rules and regulations (more than 50 per cent) for the three countries. On average, Australia had 1.4; Canada 2.1; and India 2.8 types of objective per performance audit. This compares with Australia (1.5), Canada (1.1) and India (3.5) audit objectives per audit. While more types of audit objectives for India have resulted in more audit objectives per audit, this is not true in relation to Australia and Canada. Thus, the hypothesis that on average, more types of audit objectives would necessarily mean more audit objectives per performance audit, is not supported. The types of objectives and number of objectives measure two different aspects of an audit. The types of objectives define simultaneously different types of purposes, whereas the number of objectives per audit is a measure of audit focus.

Audit approach

The observations from the content analysis on audit approaches (Table 5.2) suggest that together with 9 per cent of audits that also considered results, 100 per cent of Australian simultaneous performance audits took a system-oriented approach to performance auditing. This compares with 97 per cent of Canadian performance audits (including 18 per cent that also considered results) and

75 per cent of Indian performance audits (including 30 per cent that also considered results) took a system-oriented approach. Thus, the system-oriented approach is the dominant approach to environmental performance auditing in the three countries. Given that the environmental impact of most environmental initiatives is long-term and is not easily measurable in the short-term, it is quite logical that SAIs have taken this approach, irrespective of their individual circumstances. It is further noted that Australia leads on the system-oriented approach, with Canada also ahead of India.

A higher proportion of Indian (55 per cent – including 30 per cent that also consider systems) environmental performance audits considers direct results than does the Australian (9 per cent – which also consider systems) and Canadian (21 per cent – including 18 per cent that also consider systems) performance audits. In Australia and Canada, there appears to be a move away from direct measurement of results towards greater reliance on systems and processes. The move away from direct measurement of results towards examining the systems and processes established to achieve those results (such as reporting of achievements against key performance indicators) is a general trend in developed countries. For example, in the USA, the *Government Performance Results Act*, 1993 and in Australia, the *Public Governance, Performance and Accountability Act*, 2013 require the federal government agencies to prepare performance reports that are subjected to audit by Auditors General. There seems to be a paradigm shift from direct auditing (of results) to auditing of statements and assertions made by government agencies in such performance reports (Suzuki, 2004). This shift shows the maturity of performance auditing. Compared to India, performance auditing in Australia and Canada is considered more developed. Further, due to their longer history of reforms, public administration in Australia and Canada is more attuned to a system-approach, such as measuring their own performance and producing reports that the respective SAIs can use in their performance audits. The greater use of a system-approach in Australia and Canada than in India is consistent with the view that SAIs reflect the broader norms within the state machinery of their country (Pollitt and Summa, 1997).

Criteria

Like the audit objectives, audit criteria are a fundamental component of performance audits. Expectedly, all three SAIs have a similar notion of audit criteria as a means of measuring, judging and/or evaluating the performance of the subject matter and making them mandatory (ANAO, 2015a: 75; CAG, 2014a: 11; OAG, 2004: 52). However, the OAG's definition is more comprehensive and states that performance 'audit criteria are reasonable and attainable standards of performance *and control* against which *compliance*, *the adequacy of systems and practices*, and the economy, efficiency and cost-effectiveness of operations can be evaluated and assessed' (OAG, 2004: 52; emphasis added). The ANAO's and CAG's definitions do not include the concepts of control and compliance with the adequacy of systems and practices. These are central to the 'system-oriented' approach to performance audit that, as seen earlier (Table 5.2), is most often used by the three SAIs. The OAG (2004: 52) clearly states that 'the assessment of whether or not criteria are met results in audit observations and the aggregate of the observations enable conclusion against each audit objective. As such, it explicitly mandates the development of criteria for each line of enquiry'. On the other hand, CAG (2014a: 11) and ANAO (2015a: 75) have a general requirement for establishment of suitable criteria. As such, the ANAO (2015a: 72) and CAG (2014a: 27) requirements to conclude against each audit objective only implicitly make criteria mandatory.

The Canadian environmental performance audit reports explicitly state that the 'management reviewed and accepted the suitability of the criteria used in the audit'. This is despite the fact that only discussion, not agreement with auditees, on criteria is mandatory; however, documentation of disagreement in audit report is mandatory (OAG, 2004: 54). The Indian environmental performance audit reports sometimes refer to the entry conference, during which audit objectives and methodology were discussed (see, for example, CAG, 2013b: 7). However, they do not explicitly state whether the department(s) agreed to, or accepted, the audit criteria. The CAG (2014a: 30–31) is of the view that while the auditee's acceptance of all audit criteria is desirable and contributes to effectiveness of a performance audit, it is neither mandatory nor always possible to achieve that. However, it suggests the need for resolution of disagreements and requires the documentation of efforts to do so, but does not specify where efforts should be documented. While the Australian performance audit manual (ANAO, 2015a: 98) refers to the entry interview with auditees to discuss, among other matters, the audit objectives and criteria, it does not explicitly state that audit objectives and criteria are to be agreed by the auditees. While all Australian environmental performance audit reports had a section stating the audit objectives and criteria, none of them had any statement referring to the discussion at entry interviews about the audit objectives and criteria. Obtaining an auditee's agreement to criteria in Australia is considered not in accord with the independence of the Auditor General (McPhee, Former Auditor General of Australia, personal communication).

The observations on criteria (Table 5.2) show that only 27 per cent of Australian environmental performance audits reported audit criteria; the remaining (73 per cent) treated audit objectives/sub-objectives synonymously with the audit criteria in the reports. Further, the Australian performance audit reports also did not explicitly quote the source of audit criteria. About 9 per cent of reports indirectly referred to the sources of audit criteria. Typically, criteria in Australian performance audit reports were framed at a high level and in general terms using value-laden phrases such as whether the department 'effectively implemented the scheme' (ANAO, 2012: 16) and whether a 'structured risk management framework' was present to manage compliance risk (ANAO, 2014b: 14) without clarifying what 'effective implementation' and structured 'risk management framework' were. As such, it could be interpreted that the Australian environmental performance audits used implicit audit criteria. Wilson

(2011: 49) has also identified scope for improvement in the presentation of audit criteria in the ANAO's performance audit reports. As criteria are the basis of investigation, more criteria per objective would suggest more rigorous examination of the relevant matters, to arrive at conclusions. From this perspective, the analysis of criteria suggests that the Canadian audits (3.2 criteria per audit objective) can be considered slightly more rigorous than the Australian audits (2.6 criteria per audit objective), noting that Indian audits do not specify criteria at all (last row in Table 5.2).

The Canadian environmental performance audits always report audit criteria and source(s) of criteria in the 'About the audit' section. Where the objectives are broken down into sub-objectives, each sub-objective has its own set of criteria and sources of criteria explicitly listed. While on many occasions several audit criteria sharing the same source (legislation/policy) have created repetition, their separate listing facilitated transparency leading to better understanding. As such, this could be considered a better practice. Australian audits quote criteria and sometimes indirectly refer to sources in footnotes. However, they do not specifically mention the sources. None of the Indian environmental performance audits quote audit criteria. They only list the source of criteria – for example, legislation and policies. As such, the Indian audit could be considered as using implicit audit criteria. The lack of clearly defined audit criteria in Indian performance audits has also been noted by an international peer review (Australia et al., 2012: 28).

While the reporting of criteria is mandatory as per the reporting standards of both Australia and Canada, the Indian standard is silent on the matter. The Canadian reporting standard also mandates the reporting of sources of criteria. The reporting of criteria in the Canadian performance audits is in accord with the standard. However, the same cannot be said about the Australian performance audit reports (only 27 per cent of audits report audit criteria). The audits, not quoting the audit criteria, or the source(s) of audit criteria, do not promote transparency, which is one of the aims of auditing. While it cannot be said that the Australian and Indian environmental performance audits do not use explicit criteria, it can certainly be said that they do not always explicitly report the criteria used in the environmental performance audits. Even if their reporting standards do not require them to do so, it would be helpful if all criteria used in the Australian and Indian performance audits were explicitly stated and their sources identified. In the long term, the performance audit reporting standards ought to be enhanced and implemented rigorously to promote transparency in reporting.

Methods used for evidence collection

Compiling a list of methods used by three SAIs for collecting evidence was particularly challenging as their performance audit reports had gaps in the methodology section. The reporting of methods associated with evidence collection received inconsistent attention from the studied SAIs (Table 5.3), suggesting somewhat lesser importance being attached to it. Approximately 93 per cent of Canadian,

Table 5.3 Methods (percentage of audits) for evidence collection interpreted as used in environmental performance audits. The figures in brackets are percentage of methods used but not reported

No.	*Method*	*Australia*	*Canada*	*India*
–	Number (N) of environmental performance audits	22	30	20
–	Method section present (percentage)	91	93	40
–	Average number of methods interpreted as used	6.1	4.6	4.5
1	Document examination	100 (9)	100 (13)	100 (70)
2	Interview of officials	100 (9)	100 (13)	100 (75)
3	Survey of officials	0 (–)	7 (0)	5 (0)
4	Stakeholders consultation/survey	91 (5)	67 (5)	20 (25)
5	Site visit	50 (9)	23 (43)	75 (80)
6	Sample examination	59 (54)	23 (14)	60 (58)
7	System/process review including database	77 (59)	40 (25)	25 (100)
8	Expert opinion	9 (0)	20 (0)	10 (50)
9	Literature survey	73 (94)	37 (64)	55 (100)
10	Case study	23 (100)	13 (50)	10 (100)
11	Benchmarking	18 (75)	30 (89)	5 (100)
12	Focus group	0 (–)	0 (–)	0 (–)
13	Economical/statistical analysis	9 (100)	0 (–)	0 (–)
14	Other modelling such as hydrological, ecological	5 (100)	0 (–)	5 (100)

Source: adapted from Prasad, 2017.

91 per cent of Australian and only 40 per cent of Indian environmental performance audit reports contained a methods section. Further, Canada recognized all methods, yet reported them variously, while Australia (three) and India (five) did not recognize (used but not reported – marked 100 per cent in brackets in Table 5.3) the use of several methods including case study, economical/statistical analysis, system/process review, literature survey, benchmarking and modelling. However, this is not unusual, given that these less frequently used methods lack a consistent definition and hence are open to interpretation. The creation of a standard definition by INTOSAI on various methods would facilitate a common understanding and minimize interpretational differences.

While non-reporting of uncommon methods by some SAIs is understandable, non-reporting by all three SAIs of all methods on some occasions (even the commonly used methods, such as document examination and interview) indicates a generic gap in documentation and transparency. SAIs may argue that their audit reports are not deficient, since current standards do not mandate the inclusion of such details and their primary clients – parliamentarians – appear to show a lack of concern regarding these details. SAIs should lead by example in promoting transparency, rather than make arguments inconsistent with this ideal. Despite the maturity in the field of performance auditing and development of related standards, performance audit, unlike financial audit, is still not considered a routine exercise. Given that every performance audit is a standalone endeavour and the fundamental role methodology plays in reaching conclusions, it would be beneficial to include a methodology section in every performance audit report. Transparent reporting on each aspect of performance audit (e.g. objectives, criteria, methodology) and ensuring conclusions are aligned with objectives are critical to maintaining SAIs' reporting credibility. Establishing a reporting standard for performance audits would address this need.

The three SAIs have used 13 types of methods (Table 5.3) to collect evidence for environmental performance audits. Of all methods used, document examination and interview of officials are always (100 per cent) used by the three SAIs. These two are traditional methods relied upon by SAIs in audits, so their invariable use is expected. For Australia (91 per cent) and Canada (67 per cent), stakeholder consultation is the next highly used method, whereas for India it is site visit (75 per cent). The higher stakeholder consultation in Australia and Canada than in India (20 per cent) is consistent with the trend of more consultative governance in developed countries (Australia and Canada) compared with a developing country (India). As noted by Pollitt and Summa (1997), SAIs echo the larger tendency within the state machinery of their country.

The higher use of system and process review by Australia (77 per cent) and Canada (40 per cent) than by India (25 per cent) is consistent with the greater emphasis on the system-oriented approach to performance auditing (Table 5.2) in Australia (100 per cent) and Canada (90 per cent) than in India (75 per cent). Literature survey (37–73 per cent), site visit (23–75 per cent) and sample examination (23–60 per cent) are quite frequently used. Case study (10–23 per cent) and benchmarking (5–30 per cent) are also considerably used. Economic/statistical analysis (0–9 per cent) and modelling (0–5 per cent) are the least used methods. Canadian performance audits (30 per cent) have used benchmarking more than Australian (18 per cent) and Indian ones (5 per cent). This is quite consistent with the greater sophistication of OAG than ANAO and CAG in environmental performance auditing. The higher use of site visit in India (75 per cent) than in Australia (50 per cent) and Canada (23 per cent) is consistent with the wider mandate and institutional structure of the CAG. However, the higher use of literature survey in Indian audits than in Canadian performance audits seems to be an exception. This may be due to interpretational challenges involved when a method is not explicitly mentioned (methods interpreted as used but not reported – 100 per cent of Indian audits do not report this method compared to only 64 per cent of Canadian audits).

On average, Australia (6.1) used more methods per performance audit than Canada (4.6) and India (4.5) (Table 5.3). This is consistent with the finding in Chapter 4 that, on average, developed country SAIs use more methods for evidence collection than developing country SAIs. Further, there was more variability in the use of methods in Indian (0.4) environmental performance audits than in Australian (0.2) and Canadian (0.2) audits. Australian audit methods belonged to three classes and were mostly concentrated in two classes: 5–6 (41 per cent) and 7–8 (50 per cent). The Canadian methods also fell into three classes and are mostly concentrated in two classes: 3–4 (50 per cent) and 5–6 (43 per cent). On the other hand, the Indian audit methods were spread over five classes and most were concentrated in three classes: 3–4 (40 per cent), 5–6 (35 per cent) and 7–8 (15 per cent). While about half of the Australian and Canadian performance audits use a similar number of methods, only about 40 per cent of Indian audits use a similar number of methods. More consistency in the use of methods in Australian and Canadian performance audits indicates more consistency in the composition of their audit teams compared with composition of the Indian audit teams.

Alignment between audit objectives and conclusions

As the effectiveness of a programme is assessed by investigating whether it has met its objectives, likewise the effectiveness of a performance audit can be assessed by investigating whether the audit met its stated objective(s). In other words, the effectiveness of a performance audit process can be assessed by answering the question: Did the audit conclusion(s) address the stated audit objective(s)? Objective(s) and conclusion(s) are two fundamental characteristics of an audit that determine its effectiveness. Effectiveness in this sense – as it does not relate to measuring the impact of an audit, hence is not influenced by external factors – can be considered as an intrinsic property of an audit process itself that can also reflect audit quality. This property is the alignment between each objective and conclusion that can be estimated as a rule-based index varying continuously between 0 (no alignment) and 1 (perfect alignment).

All three SAIs' performance audit standards/manuals prescribe that a performance audit must conclude against each of its objectives. However, environmental performance audits of all three SAIs did not always meet this requirement. Only 32 per cent of Australian, 93 per cent of Canadian and 15 per cent of Indian environmental performance audits (Figure 5.1) achieved an alignment between 0.9 and 1, meriting them being considered as well-aligned audits that either directly or closely concluded against all their objectives. About 10 per cent of Australian and 35 per cent of Indian environmental performance audits (Figure 5.1) did not conclude against their objectives. In these cases, either the audit objectives were not defined clearly, or the conclusions did not address the stated objectives, or both.

A statistical analysis reveals that the mean alignment index for Canada was 1; for Australia 0.7; and for India 0.5. This suggests that, on average, the Canadian environmental performance audit conclusions are almost perfectly aligned with their objectives, while about 70 per cent aligned for the Australian performance audits, and only about half aligned for the Indian performance audits. With almost negligible coefficient of variation, Canadian environment performance audits were most consistent in making a conclusion against objectives. With a coefficient of variation of 0.9, the Indian performance audits were least consistent in making a conclusion against objectives. With a coefficient of variation

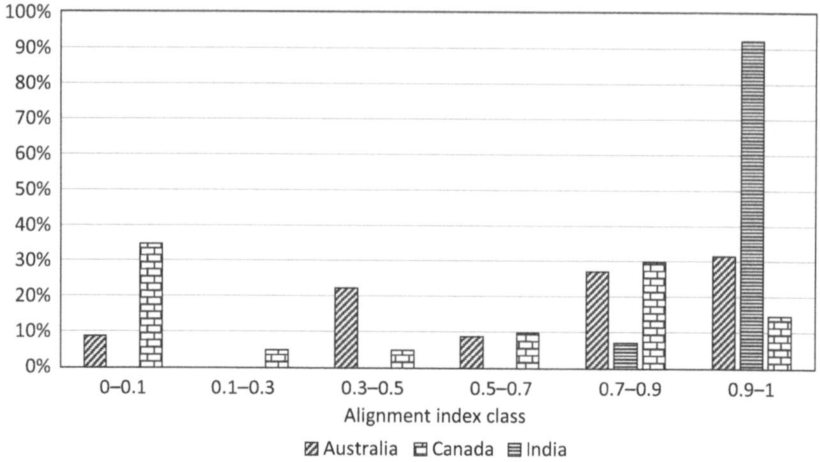

Figure 5.1 Frequency distribution of alignment index. In this graph, 0 indicates no alignment and 1 indicates a perfect (1:1) alignment between performance audit objective(s) and conclusions.

Source: after Prasad, 2017.

of 0.4, the Australian performance audits consistency in concluding against audit objectives also significantly varied. The results suggest that Canada has taken the most disciplined and methodological approach to environment performance auditing, whereas Australia and India, while endeavouring to do a good job in the circumstances, have scope for improvement. An international peer review (Australia et. al, 2012: 29) has recommended improvement in the Indian performance audit design by refining the development of audit objective, audit criteria and test programmes.

Concluding against objectives is a major decision in a performance audit process that is reviewed several times before the audit is finalized. Therefore it is highly unlikely that conclusions not matching objectives is due to any omission. It is quite possible that Auditors General prefer not to frame their conclusions in 'black and white', or sometimes conclusions are very difficult to summarize/reduce to the precise wordings of audit objectives. It is also recognized that objectives, and hence conclusions, might change during an audit due to the discovery of new facts or new circumstances. However, in such cases, the objectives should be amended and conclusions made against new objectives rather than leaving objectives intact and creating a misalignment between conclusions and objectives.

Performance audit recommendations

Performance audits, in addition to promoting accountability, are mainly aimed at improving performance of government entities. As such, performance

Table 5.4 Recommendations made in environmental performance audits

Matter	*Australia*	*Canada*	*India*
Number (N) of performance audits	22	28	20
Number of recommendations	43	121	173
Average number of recommendations per audit	2.0	4.3	8.7
Should/recommends (%)	100	100	39
Need (%)	–	–	29
Essential/important (%)	–	–	2
Advisable (%)	–	–	1
May/could (%)	–	–	29
Audits using the same verb in all recommendations (%)	100	100	35
Responsible actor identified (%)	100	100	61
Entity/department (%)	100	100	24
Government (%)	–	–	37
Entities responded	100	100	0
Recommendations accepted (%)	100	98	–

audits should include recommendations for actions that will bring significant improvements in performance (ANAO, 2015a: 170; OAG, 2004: 68). Recommendations should address the causes, not the symptoms, of the issues. They generally are aimed at addressing strategic issues and serious deficiencies, not each audit finding (OAG, 2004: 68). In some circumstances, for example relating to routine operational matters, a recommendation is not the best way to achieve the intended result. A discussion with the audited entity may produce a better result – for example, a suggested change in routine business processes that promotes efficiency might be immediately implemented.

On average, Australian (2.0) environmental performance audits made fewer recommendations per audit than the Canadian (4.3) and Indian (8.7) audits (Table 5.4). About 20 per cent of Australian performance audits made no recommendations at all. A further analysis of the data finds that only 40 per cent of Indian performance audits have made 0–4 recommendations, while the remaining 60 per cent have made five or more recommendations. This compares with about 90 per cent of Australian audits and 60 per cent of Canadian audits making 0–4 recommendations. This would suggest there are systemic preferences for larger numbers of audit recommendations in India than in Australia and Canada. This may be reflective of the nature of the relationship between the CAG and the administration in India. Compared with Australia and Canada, the relationship between the audit office and government administration in India is still cast in a traditional mode, which to some extent can be termed adversarial.

Fewer recommendations could suggest a greater focus on important strategic issues. There is a near consensus among SAIs that recommendations should add value and not every issue discussed in an audit warrants a recommendation. The

ANAO does not recommend an existing requirement, as it considers it does not add any value. The Australian and Canadian environmental performance audits always (100 per cent) direct their recommendations to specific entity(ies) making consistent use of verbs ('recommends' or 'should') in all their recommendations (Table 5.4). On the other hand, Indian environmental performance audit recommendations use a variety of verbs ('should' (39 per cent); 'need' (29 per cent); 'is essential/important' (2 per cent); 'is advisable' (1 per cent); and 'may/could' (29 per cent)), and in only about 60 per cent of cases identified entity(ies) responsible for actions, though required under the Indian performance audit manual (CAG, 2014a: 43). This suggests a somewhat lesser degree of quality control in Indian performance audit reports.

In all (100 per cent) Australian and Canadian performance audit reports, the government agencies formally responded to the recommendations indicating their clear agreement or disagreement with the audit recommendations. All (100 per cent) Australian and 98 per cent of Canadian environmental performance audit recommendations were accepted by the relevant government agencies. On the other hand, none (0 per cent) of the Indian environmental performance audit reports contained any formal response by the government agencies. Consequently, it was not clear how many CAG environmental performance audit recommendations were accepted. Unlike in Australia and Canada, routine responses to performance audit recommendations in India are followed up by the PAC of the legislature through a review of action taken notes by departments that are largely unresponsive. This has created a heavy burden on the PAC. Extremely concerned with the situation, the PAC of the Indian parliament established a sub-committee to investigate the matter (CAG, 2010b: 6). Legislative changes to the CAG's *Duties, Powers and Conditions of Service Act, 1971* were proposed in 2009 to expand the mandate of the CAG with the aim, among others, to improve the timeliness of response by the audited entities (Australia et al., 2012: 31). As of December 2017, these changes were yet to be legislated.

Comment on policy matters

Sharing the common heritage of the Westminster system of governance, the three SAIs serve their respective parliaments (though the Indian SAI is established by the Constitution itself, not by an Act of parliament). In the Westminster system, the supremacy of the legislature (parliament) in setting policy is well recognized. Even under the separation of powers doctrine, the judiciary only decides the legality of policies/legislation, not their merit. While the enabling legislative provisions do not explicitly prohibit the three SAIs from considering or commenting on the policy matters, they generally do not do so as a matter of high regard for the established convention of supremacy of the parliament. The three SAIs explicitly declare their position on the matter in publicly available documents. For example, the ANAO (2015b: 2) states that it 'does not comment on the merits of government policy'. The OAG in all its performance audit reports (e.g. OAG, 2014e: ii) declares that while it 'may comment on policy implementation in a performance audit, it does not comment on the merits of a policy'. The CAG (2014a: 5) states that its performance audit 'does not question the intentions and decisions of the legislature, but examines whether any shortcomings in the laws and regulations or their way of implementation have prevented the specified objectives from being achieved'. The CAG's position is interesting as it highlights the grey area of separation between so-called 'black and white' policy and policy implementation that performance audits sometimes entail. A serving Auditor General of Australia has observed that in situations incidental to a performance audit, if the ANAO finds that aspects of a government policy would benefit from a review, it has recommended departments consider the position and advise the government accordingly. This is a responsible position for the ANAO to take in such circumstances (McPhee, 2011: 7). The OAG (2004: 14–15) explicitly acknowledges the relationship between the audit function and government policy and policy making. It has devoted a full section in its performance audit manual, where it also refers to a discussion paper prepared to provide additional information on the relationship between policy and auditing. The OAG (2004: 14–15) further observes that, when it needs to comment on the adequacy of government policy, its risk increases when it moves from the routine administrative areas (such as service delivery and contract administration) to more political areas needing specific policy decisions, programmes or policy goals (such as closing certain government offices, fishery conservation policy and reducing child poverty).

The main point to note from the above discussion is that, occasionally, the performance audit needs to comment on government policy, especially on its adequacy or absence. For example, the ANAO in one of its politically sensitive performance audits noted: 'There are important lessons here for those agencies with policy implementation responsibilities but also those *responsible for policy development*' (ANAO, 2010b: 27; emphasis added).

The OAG (2011a: 24), in one of its studies, virtually reminded parliamentarians of their responsibilities, encouraging them to ask questions such as:

- What specific legislative and policy tools are needed to address current and emerging issues, such as international management of fisheries, marine protected areas, and eco-certification?
- What steps are being taken to put those tools in place?
- What legislative and policy safeguards have been put in place to ensure that fisheries decisions respect the scientifically determined ecological limits? What is the evidence that these safeguards are working as intended?

Though not technically audits, the studies are like performance audits in all respects except for the lack of criteria, and they do provide the framework and criteria for future audits (OAG, 2011a: 1). It can be argued that, through this study, the OAG has almost entered into a political debate on policy matters. This is not inconsistent with the position of the OAG on policy matters, as noted earlier.

The CAG in India has been proactive in its work. Its proactive stance on the environment almost venturing into the policy domain can be understood from the following statement made in an audit report (CAG, 2010b: i, 1):

> Protection and conservation of the environment is increasingly becoming important, especially in light of observed climate change which has devastating consequences for the survival of humanity. In this context, effective environmental governance by the Executive is of utmost importance. … Our objective, through this report, is to create awareness and urgency about conservation and protection of the environment which need to be addressed by the Government. … The report would also help in sensitising policy makers to look at environmental issues with a holistic approach and address deficiencies in programs/schemes/policies so that our environment is conserved more effectively.

In another example of entry into the policy domain in India, the CAG (2011a: viii) identified several weaknesses in legislative and policy frameworks, noting that:

> Water pollution has not been adequately addressed in any policy in India, both at the central and the State level. In the absence of a specific water pollution policy which would also incorporate prevention of pollution, treatment of polluted water and ecological restoration of polluted water bodies, government efforts in these areas would not get the required emphasis and thrust.

It is clear from the above discussion that, notwithstanding their general position of not commenting on the merits of policies, the three SAIs have not shied away from entering into the policy domain. While the OAG and CAG stance on policy has been more proactive, that of the ANAO has been somewhat circumspect.

Tone and tenor of environmental performance audit reports

An audit report is considered balanced if it does not solely focus on criticizing identified lack of performance, but contains a fair assessment that also acknowledges good performance (CAG, 2014a: 59). Balanced reporting of an audit is stressed by all three SAIs in their performance audit guidelines and manuals (ANAO, 2015a: 163–164; CAG, 2014a: 17; OAG, 2004: 76).

The tone of all Australian and Canadian environmental performance audit reports reviewed herein was considered balanced and positive. However, the tone of some Indian performance audit reports could be considered somewhat adversarial. They used combative phrases such as 'the department stated' to describe the department's position and 'was not acceptable' to describe its disagreement (see, for example, CAG, 2011b: 19, 22; 2013c: 31). This may be compared with the use of softer/neutral phrases, such as the officials/department 'informed'/'we found' and 'we could not agree' to describe the equivalent situations in Australian and Canadian environmental performance audit reports (see, for example, OAG, 2010a: 10; 2010b: 24; ANAO, 2012: 24; 2014b: 89). One CAG report used the phrase 'lackadaisical approach' (CAG, 2013e: 19) to describe omissions by the department. An international peer review of the CAG noted that, of the 35-sample audit reports it reviewed, about half could have been more balanced in content and tone (Australia et al., 2012: 19). In this context, the review cited the then CAG's Auditing Standards requirement that the use of language that generates defensiveness and opposition should be avoided (CAG, 2002: 31).

The peer review also noted that, as a large number of government projects were 'beset by substantial time and cost overruns, and poor outcomes' (Australia et. al., 2012: 16), there were often considerable deficiencies in programme administration and implementation for the Indian SAI to report (Australia et al., 2012: 36). It is interesting to note that, compared with 32 per cent of Australian and 54 per cent of Canadian environmental performance audits, 100 per cent of the Indian environmental performance audits found that government programmes either did not have the requisite systems and processes to achieve their objectives, or did not achieve their objectives. In describing the deficiencies, on average the language of the ANAO can be considered soft (see, for example, ANAO, 2014a: 24; 2014b: 18); that of the OAG can be considered firm (see, for example, OAG, 2010c: 30; 2011c: 16; 2014f: 32); and that of the CAG can be considered strong (see, for example, CAG, 2011c: 70, 72, 73, 77; 2013a: vi). This book does not defend the use of strong language, especially when it is not sanctioned by the relevant standards. However, there appears to be a correlation between the overall effectiveness of administration in programme implementation and the degree of softness in language – the higher the overall effectiveness of administration in implementing the environmental programmes, the softer the tone of the performance audit reports in pointing out the deficiencies and vice versa. This puts the tone of the language used by the three SAIs in their performance audit reports in context.

Deficient monitoring and reporting: a common finding

A finding common between the three countries has been that the majority (65–85 per cent) of environmental performance audits have identified issues with data, monitoring and reporting of the implementation of environmental policies, programmes and projects. The Australian environmental performance audit reports frequently raised issues about development and reporting of performance measures, such as key performance indicators for environmental programmes. On the other hand, the emphasis of Canadian audit reports has been on the collection and reporting of environmental data. The Indian audit reports were more concerned with the basic monitoring of projects, though some (e.g. CAG, 2011a) also raised concerns with monitoring and reporting of environmental data.

Conclusion

The results of a comparative study of environmental performance auditing in Australia, Canada and India suggest that while the three SAIs have adequate QMFs in place, the quality of their reports varies, not just between them, but also within them. On almost all aspects studied, the Indian environmental audit reports, when compared to those of the Australian and Canadian SAIs, illustrated more variability. This could, in part, be attributed to the Indian SAI possessing a wider jurisdiction, complex institutional arrangements, less prescriptive auditing standards and variable quality of supervision. However, although the Australian and Canadian SAIs are characterized as having a much narrower jurisdiction, less complex institutional arrangements and more prescriptive standards, significant inconsistency was also present in their audit reports. This inconsistency points to some generic underlying causes, one of which, and perhaps the most plausible, is that performance audits reporting is not receiving due attention. This is an area that the SAI community through INTOSAI could address.

Note

1 The earlier version of the Indian standards noted that 'the standards are meant to assist, not to supersede the prudent judgement of the Auditor in making audit observations, conclusions and report' (CAG, 2002: 30). The earlier version further conceded that unlike financial audit reports, performance audit reports are varied in content (CAG, 2002: 39).

References

ANAO. (2010a). *The Auditor-General Annual Report 2009–10*. Canberra: ANAO.

ANAO. (2010b). *Home Insulation Program*, Audit Report 12. Canberra: ANAO.

ANAO. (2012). *Administration of the National Greenhouse and Energy Reporting Scheme*, Audit Report 23. Canberra: ANAO.

ANAO. (2014a). *Establishment and Administration of the National Offshore Petroleum Safety and Environmental Management Authority*, Report 38. Canberra: ANAO.

ANAO. (2014c). *Managing Compliance with EPBC Act 1999 Conditions of Approval*, Report 43. Canberra: ANAO.

ANAO. (2015a). *Performance Audit Manual*. Canberra: ANAO.

ANAO. (2015b). *Guidelines for the Conduct of Performance Audits*. Canberra: ANAO.

ANAO. (2016a). Performance audits: open for contribution. Retrieved 20 January 2016 from www.anao.gov.au/work-program/contribute.

AUASB. (2008). *ASAE 3500*. Melbourne: Australian Auditing and Assurance Standard Board.

Australia (ANAO), Canada (OAG), Denmark (R), The Netherlands (AR) & United States of America (GAO). (2012). *International Peer Review of the Supreme Audit Institution of India*. New Delhi: Comptroller and Auditor General of India.
Australia (ANAO), The Netherlands (AR), Denmark (R), Sweden (R) & Norway (R) (2010). *International Peer Review of the Office of the Auditor General of Canada*. Ottawa: Office of the Auditor General of Canada.
CAG. (2002). *Indian Audit and Accounts Department Auditing Standards* (2nd edn). New Delhi: Comptroller and Auditor General of India.
CAG. (2010a). *Environment and Climate Change: Auditing Guidelines*. New Delhi: Comptroller and Auditor General of India.
CAG. (2010b). *Audit of Department of Environment and Forests*, Report 17. New Delhi: Comptroller and Auditor General of India.
CAG. (2011a). *Performance Audit of Water Pollution in India*, Report 21. New Delhi: Comptroller and Auditor General of India.
CAG. (2011b). *Protection and Conservation of Forests in Goa*, Audit Report. New Delhi: Comptroller and Auditor General of India.
CAG. (2011c). *Management of Dal Lake*, Audit Report. New Delhi: Comptroller and Auditor General of India.
CAG. (2013a). *Compensatory Afforestation in India*, Report No 21. New Delhi: Comptroller and Auditor General of India.
CAG. (2013b). *Performance Audit on Disaster Preparedness in India*, Report 5. New Delhi: Comptroller and Auditor General of India.
CAG. (2013c). *Performance Audit on Management of Bio-Medical Waste in Government-Sector Hospitals*. New Delhi: Comptroller and Auditor General of India.
CAG. (2013d). Environment audit. Asian Journal of Government Audit, 9, 19.
CAG. (2013e). *Performance Audit on Protection of Forests and Wildlife of Rajasthan*, Audit Report. New Delhi: Comptroller and Auditor General of India.
CAG. (2014a). *Performance Auditing Guidelines, 2014*. New Delhi: Comptroller and Auditor General of India.
CAG. (2014b). *Comptroller & Auditor General of India's Performance Report 2013–14*. New Delhi: Comptroller and Auditor General of India.
CAG. (2014c). *Audit Quality Management Framework*. New Delhi: Comptroller and Auditor General of India.
CAG. (2017). CAG's Auditing Standards (3rd edn). Retrieved 6 December 2017 from www.saiindia.gov.in/sites/default/files/cag_pdf/Auditing_Standards_new.pdf.
Dowdeswell, E., Mitchell, J. & Ogilvie, K. (2007). *Fulfilling the Potential: A Review of the Environment and Sustainable Development Practice of the Office of the Auditor General of Canada*. Ottawa: The Independent Green Ribbon Panel, Office of the Auditor General of Canada.
INTOSAI. (2004). *Performance Audit Guidelines: ISSAI 3000–3100*. Stockholm: INTOSAI.
McGlashan, L. (2014). *The Office of the Auditor General of Canada: Beyond Bean Counting*. Ottawa: Library of Parliament.
McPhee, I. (2011). The evolving role and mandate of the ANAO since federation. Paper presented at the Senate Occasional Lecture, Parliament House, Canberra. www.anao.gov.au/sites/g/files/net616/f/McPhee_Evolving_Role_and_Mandate_2011.pdf
OAG. (2004). *Performance Audit Manual*. Ottawa: Office of the Auditor General of Canada.
OAG. (2010a). Scientific research: agriculture and agri-food Canada. In *The Spring 2010 Report of the Auditor General of Canada*. Ottawa: Office of the Auditor General of Canada.

OAG. (2010b). Oil spills from ships. In *The Fall 2010 Report of the Commissioner of Environment and Sustainable Development*. Ottawa: Office of the Auditor General of Canada.

OAG. (2010c). Sustaining development in the Northwest Territories. In *The Spring 2010 Report of the Auditor General of Canada*. Ottawa: Office of the Auditor General of Canada.

OAG. (2011a). Study of managing fisheries for sustainability. In *The December 2011 Commissioner of the Environment and Sustainable Development Report*. Ottawa: Office of the Auditor General of Canada.

OAG. (2011b). *4th E Practice Guide: Integrating Environmental Considerations in Performance Audit Work*. Ottawa: Office of the Auditor General of Canada.

OAG. (2011c). Climate change plans under the Kyoto Protocol Implementation Act. In *The Fall Report of the Commissioner of the Environment and Sustainable Development 2011*. Ottawa: Office of the Auditor General of Canada.

OAG. (2014a). Performance audit – exhibit – OAG performance audit planning. Retrieved 11 January 2016 from www.oag-bvg.gc.ca/internet/methodology/performance-audit/manual/18915_ENC_INTERNET_QA.shtm.

OAG. (2014b). Selection of audit topics. Retrieved 10 January 2016 from www.oag-bvg.gc.ca/internet/methodology/performance-audit/manual/1510.shtm.

OAG. (2014c). Acquiring and maintaining knowledge of business. Retrieved 22 November 2015 from www.oag-bvg.gc.ca/internet/methodology/performance-audit/manual/1505.shtm.

OAG. (2014d). Audit criteria. Retrieved 22 November 2015 from www.oag-bvg.gc.ca/internet/methodology/performance-audit/manual/4043.shtm.

OAG. (2014e). Environmental monitoring of oil sands. In *Report of the Commissioner of the Environment and Sustainable Development*. Ottawa: Office of the Auditor General of Canada.

OAG. (2014f). Environmental and social review at Export Development Canada. In *The Fall Report of the Commissioner of the Environment and Sustainable Development*. Ottawa: Office of the Auditor General of Canada.

OAG. (2014g). Who we are. Retrieved 23 July 2014 from www.oag-bvg.gc.ca/internet/English/au_fs_e_370.html#Commissioner

OECD. (2004). *Environmental Performance Reviews – Canada*. Paris: OECD.

Pollitt, C. & Summa, H. (1997). Reflexive watchdogs? How supreme audit institutions account for themselves. *Public Administration*, 75(2), 313–336.

Prasad, A. (2017). Environmental performance auditing in Australia, Canada and India. *International Journal of Government Auditing*, 44(2), 24–26

Prasad, A. (2016). *Environmental Performance Auditing by Supreme Audit Institutions: Progress, Practice and Prospects*. PhD thesis, The Australian National University, Canberra. Retrieved 15 April 2017 from http://hdl.handle.net/1885/112881.

Rose, G. (2001). Environmental performance auditing of government: the role for an Australian Commissioner for the Environment. *Environmental and Planning Law Journal*, 18(3), 293–318.

Suzuki, Y. (2004). Basic structure of government auditing by a supreme audit institution. *Government Auditing Review*, 11, 39–53.

WGEA. (2004). *Fourth Survey on Environmental Auditing* Stockholm: INTOSAI Working Group on Environmental Auditing.

WGEA. (2007). *Fifth Survey on Environmental Auditing*: Stockholm: INTOSAI Working Group on Environmental Auditing.

WGEA. (2012). *Seventh Survey on Environmental Auditing*: Stockholm: INTOSAI Working Group on Environmental Auditing.

Wilkins, P. & Boyle, R. (2011). Standards and quality. In J. Lonsdale, P. Wilkins and T. Ling (Eds), *Performance Auditing: Contributing to Accountability in Democratic Government* (pp. 147–171). Cheltenham: Edward Elgar.

Wilson, G. (2011). *Planning and Scoping of Performance Audits*. Canberra: Australian National Audit Office.

6 Challenges and barriers

The matters discussed in earlier chapters were largely related to environmental performance auditing or to Supreme Audit Institutions (SAIs) themselves. However, performance auditing, like most other government endeavours, requires resources to undertake and faces challenges and barriers. In many cases, these challenges and barriers affect their activities, but are outside the control of SAIs. The Working Group on Environmental Auditing (WGEA) has been collecting data on barriers to environmental auditing in its tri-annual surveys of SAIs. Further, data on barriers and challenges were collected as part of the survey discussed in Chapter 4. The discussion in this chapter on challenges and barriers faced in undertaking environmental performance auditing is based upon both sources of data.

Long-term nature of environmental policies and programmes

As noted in Chapter 2, notwithstanding their views that environmental audit is no different from audits in other fields (INTOSAI, 2012; Van Leeuwen, 2004; Yusoff, 2013), SAIs do identify a number of challenges specific to environmental auditing (INTOSAI, 2012). One such challenge is the long-term nature of environmental problems and associated initiatives to respond to them. An overwhelming majority (about 90 per cent) of SAIs (Figure 6.1) agree that the long-term nature of some environmental programmes and policies pose particular challenges to performance auditing. Only a minority (about 10 per cent) of SAIs disagree. About 10 per cent more developing country SAIs than the developed SAIs (83 per cent) agree that the long-term nature of some environmental policies pose challenges to performance auditing. Developed SAIs, due to their comparatively greater resource endowment, expertise and experience in undertaking performance audit of environmental matters, are less likely to consider them as posing specific challenges. The difference between their responses is consistent with expectations. The more notable point here is that an overwhelming majority of SAIs do recognize that the long-term nature of some environmental initiatives pose challenges to performance auditing. Barrett (Former Auditor General of Australia, personal communication) notes, however, that it is not a problem unique to the environment sector.

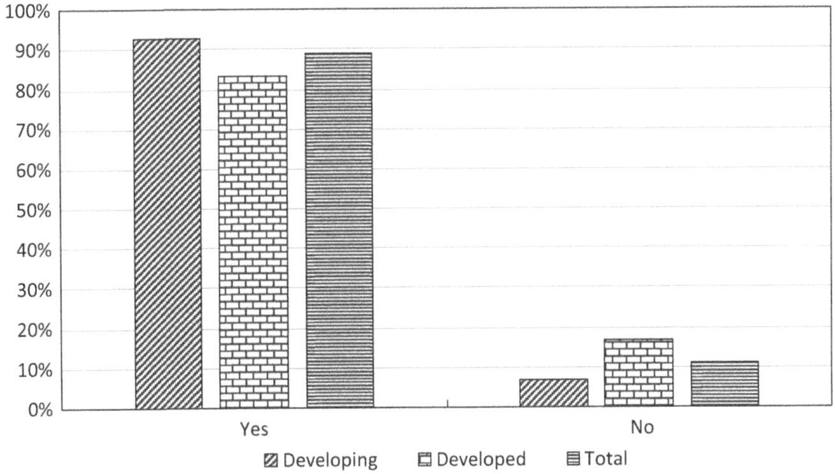

Figure 6.1 Does the long-term nature of the outcome of some environmental programmes/policies pose particular challenges to the performance audit, for example in assessing effectiveness? Response (percentage) – developing SAIs (N = 28); developed SAIs (N = 18); total SAIs (N = 46).

Barriers to environmental auditing

The following are the most common barriers to environmental auditing identified by the WGEA. Questions related to these have been asked in most WGEA surveys. The barriers have been abbreviated as noted in the brackets to fit them in tables and graphs:

- lack of skills or expertise within the SAI (Skills);
- insufficient data on the state of the environment (Data);
- insufficient monitoring and reporting systems (Mon & rep);
- insufficient formulation of government environmental policy, such as goals that are not measurable, absence of a strategy or insufficient regulatory framework (Policy);
- insufficient established environmental norms and standards (Norms & stds);
- inadequate SAI mandate (Mandate); and
- other.

The following three additional factors were identified in the 2012 survey (WGEA, 2012a):

- lack of human resources (Resources);
- lack of environmental programmes (Programmes); and
- lack of technical resources (e.g. insufficient equipment and poor internet connection) (Technical).

While it may be argued that a lack of human resources could be considered part of the skills factors, WGEA has considered it worthy of a separate factor, as this may be related to the sheer number of people available within the SAIs. Identification of lack of environmental programmes to audit is an interesting factor to note. It may not in itself reflect any deficiency in SAIs. However, when it comes to measuring and reporting their outputs in terms of environmental audits as compared to their peers, it becomes an issue.

Table 6.1 summarizes the data on barriers to environmental auditing collected by the WGEA in its triennial surveys. The table also lists the response to the three new factors that were raised for the first time in the 2012 survey. Some caution is required in interpreting trends in the survey data, as respondents vary between surveys (there was an overlap of 71 per cent between the 2009 and 2012 surveys (WGEA, 2012c: 38); and of 79 per cent between the 2003 and 2006 surveys (WGEA, 2007: 60–61)); however, the response percentage of the core set of countries that participated in all surveys is indeterminate due to unavailability of individual responses). With these limitations, the data in Table 6.1 show that the following have been consistently identified by SAIs as the three most frequently encountered barriers to environmental auditing: (1) a lack of skills or expertise within SAIs; (2) insufficient data on the state of the environment; and (3) insufficient monitoring and reporting systems. If an SAI has a mandate to audit, and there is some environmental programme to audit, these three factors form the basic questions about the audit: (1) does the SAI have the necessary skill/expertise to undertake the audit (including the capacity to engage with auditees); (2) is there sufficient information available to audit; and (3) are there sufficient systems and processes in place to get data and information on an ongoing basis? As environmental policies and programmes, generally, are long-term endeavours, their audit generally would require long-term monitoring. The latter two questions that relate to this issue are within the purview of auditees, not of SAIs.

Concerns about the top three barriers listed above are greater in OLACEFS[1] and ARABOSAI than in other INTOSAI regions; they are lower in CAROSAI and EUROSAI than in other regions (Table 6.2). Temporally, of the three top barriers, concerns about the lack of skills/expertise remain high but static. On the other hand, concerns about the data and monitoring are growing. Even in developed regions – Europe and Northern America, where concerns about a lack of skills as a barrier are quite low – SAIs' concerns about insufficient data on the state of the environment and inadequate monitoring and reporting systems are growing.

The next most frequently faced barrier is a lack of details in environmental policies (Table 6.1). It is not uncommon that environmental policies are insufficiently formulated, with the result that they have vague or all-encompassing aspirational goals that cannot be measured; they lack a strategy for implementation; have unclear roles and responsibilities; and they do not sufficiently

Table 6.1 Most common barriers to environmental auditing (percentage of SAIs giving 'yes' response). The barriers are abbreviated and shows a lack of or deficiency in the abbreviated item

Barriers	*1997(N = 79)*	*2000(N = 105)*	*2003(N = 114)*	*2006(N = 79)*	*2009(N = 106)*	*2012(N = 112)*	*Average*
Skills	–	50	58	56	58	59	56
Data	41	37	40	51	62	66	51
Mon & rep	51	39	40	41	68	65	51
Policy	–	26	31	40	52	57	41
Norms & stds	49	35	40	35	52	37	40
Mandate	22	26	25	22	21	11	21
Other	30	11	9	6	30	12	14
Resources	–	–	–	–	–	65	65
Programmes	–	–	–	–	–	30	30
Technical	–	–	–	–	–	29	29

Source: WGEA after Prasad, 2018.

Table 6.2 Ranking (based upon average of three WGEA surveys – 2006, 2009 and 2012) of barriers to environmental auditing among INTOSAI regions (1 means higher rank and shows comparatively greater concerns, 7 shows comparatively lower concerns among INTOSAI regions)

INTOSAI region	*Skills/expertise*	*Env. data*	*Mon & report syst*	*Env policy*	*Env norms & stds*	*SAI mandate*	*Overall sum*	*Overall rank*
ARABOSAI	1	2	2	6	1	2	14	1
OLACEFS	2	1	1	1	4	6	15	2
PASAI	5	3	4	2	2	3	19	3
ASOSAI	4	4	5	3	5	4	25	4
AFROSAI	6	5	3	4	3	5	26	5
CAROSAI	3	7	7	7	7	1	32	6
EUROSAI	7	6	6	5	6	7	37	7

Note: data for the Others region (USA and Canada) are available only for 2009 and 2012 surveys, so this region is not ranked and included.

specify a regulatory framework. There may be reasons for this so-called 'constructive ambiguity'. Environmental problems, being socio-economic, involve numerous stakeholders, who sometimes hold diametrically opposing views. To bring the maximum number of stakeholders on board and move forward, sometimes governments must craft environmental policies in a quite ambivalent way. Perhaps having an imperfect and insufficiently detailed policy is considered a better alternative than no policy at all. Democratic governments all over the world face this sort of stark choice in contentious policy areas such as the environment. While this explains the reasons for insufficiently detailed environmental policies, this does make the work of SAIs harder when it comes to auditing the implementation of those policies. As auditing involves comparing what 'should be' with 'what is', not knowing from the policy what 'should be' makes it harder to audit. Concerns about the details of environmental policies are higher in OLACEFS and PASAI and lower in CAROSAI and EUROSAI than in other regions (Table 6.2). Surprisingly, SAIs of USA and Canada,[2] are also highly concerned about this factor. In terms of temporal trend, globally increasing numbers of SAIs are reporting that insufficiently detailed environmental policies are a barrier to environmental auditing.

The environmental norms and standards reflect social values about the environment that are codified in some professional or even legal documents. They also guide the SAIs in formulating the criteria for environmental audits. The mandate is the power of an SAI to conduct the audit. On average, a smaller proportion of SAIs consider environmental norms and standards and mandate as barriers to environmental auditing (Table 6.1). These two factors also exhibit a temporally decreasing trend. Environmental norms and standards are a matter of greater concern in ARABOSAI and PASAI and of lower concern in CAROSAI and EUROSAI than in other regions (Table 6.2). Surprisingly, either Canada or the USA is also concerned about environmental norms and standards and considers it to be a barrier to environmental auditing. The WGEA has consistently maintained that SAIs' existing mandates are considered sufficient to undertake environmental audits. Despite this, a significantly large proportion of SAIs in CAROSAI and ARABOSAI regions still consider it as a barrier to environmental auditing.

Of the newly identified barriers in the 2012 WGEA survey (WGEA, 2012a), the lack of human resources is considered as a barrier by about two-thirds of SAIs (Table 6.1). This is as high as the concern for inadequate monitoring and reporting systems in that survey. The majority of SAIs in all regions except Europe (46 per cent) consider it a barrier to environmental auditing (WGEA, 2012a: 69). The concern for this factor is higher in PASAI (89 per cent), CAROSAI (83 per cent) and OLACEFS (80 per cent) than in other regions (WGEA, 2012a: 69). Surprisingly, either the USA or Canada is also concerned about this matter (WGEA, 2012a: 69). About one-third of SAIs (Table 6.1) consider the lack of environmental programmes (30 per cent) and lack of technical resources (29 per cent) as barriers to environmental auditing. The concern for a lack of environmental programmes is greater in ARABOSAI (56 per cent) and PASAI (56 per cent) than in other regions (WGEA, 2012a: 70). For some regions (e.g. EUORSAI, CAROSAI), either it is not a concern, or a concern to a very low proportion of SAIs. This is also not a concern either to the USA or Canada (WGEA, 2012a: 70). About half of SAIs in AFROSAI (52 per cent) and PASAI (44 per cent) perhaps lack physical resources such as equipment and internet; therefore, they consider these as barriers to environmental auditing (WGEA, 2012a: 70). The low- or middle-income status of most of the countries in these regions explain the dearth of physical resources there, and hence their concern for these factors as barriers to environmental auditing.

All of the above barriers to environmental auditing are more so for environmental performance auditing as this form of auditing is more resource-intensive – both in terms of skills and data – than purely regularity (financial and compliance) environmental auditing that contributes to total environmental auditing.

Barriers to cooperation between SAIs

An overwhelmingly large proportion of SAIs indicate in: (a) WGEA surveys-96 per cent (N = 53) in the 2009 survey (WGEA, 2009: 20) and 97 per cent (N = 74) in the 2012 survey (WGEA, 2012a: 32)); and (b) the survey for this study described in Chapter 4, that cooperation has been useful. Despite its acknowledged benefits, cooperation is not always occurring, as many SAIs face several barriers to cooperation (Table 6.3). Lack of resources, lack of skills within the SAI and lack of partners for cooperation are the three top barriers to cooperation. Lack of resources, including lack of expertise, is the most frequently encountered barrier to environmental auditing (Table 6.1). This becomes more acute in the case of cooperation with other SAIs, as resources are required to coordinate and facilitate the cooperation activity, in addition to undertaking an

Table 6.3 Barriers to cooperation (percentage of SAIs)

No.	*Reasons of cooperation not occurring*	*2006 (N = 119)*	*2009 (N = 52)*	*2012 (N = 37)*	*Average*
1	Lack of resources	45	31	62	46
2	Lack of skills or expertise within SAI	35	33	51	40
3	Lack of partners	19	21	27	22
4	Inadequate SAI mandate	22	15	14	17
5	Lack of interest in SAI	8	2	5	5
6	No perceived need for cooperation	–	–	14	14
7	N/A or others	8	4	24	12

Source: WGEA.

audit. Other reasons for cooperation not occurring are: inadequate SAI mandate and lack of interest in SAIs. The WGEA 2012 survey (WGEA, 2012a: 71) listed 'no perceived need for cooperation' as another reason.

A ranking analysis (Prasad, 2016: 126) of the top three barriers to cooperation across in the INTOSAI regions suggested that:

- compared with the other regions, the SAIs in the EUORSAI region perceived lower barriers to cooperation;
- compared with the other regions, the SAIs in the PASAI region perceived greater barriers to cooperation; and
- CAROSAI was the next region after PASAI that perceives greater barriers to cooperation.

Compared with other regions, the SAIs in the EUROSAI region are generally more resourceful and perhaps the European Union also provides a more conducive context for cooperation. Therefore, these SAIs perceive lesser barriers to cooperation than other regions.

Environmental auditing capacity and resources

SAI environmental auditing budget and their output of environmental performance audits

Lack of skills (capacity) is a major barrier to environmental auditing. The SAIs' budget may be considered as a broad indicator of its environmental audit capacity. There is almost an exponential relationship between the proportion of SAIs' budget spent on environmental auditing (WGEA, 2012a) and their environmental

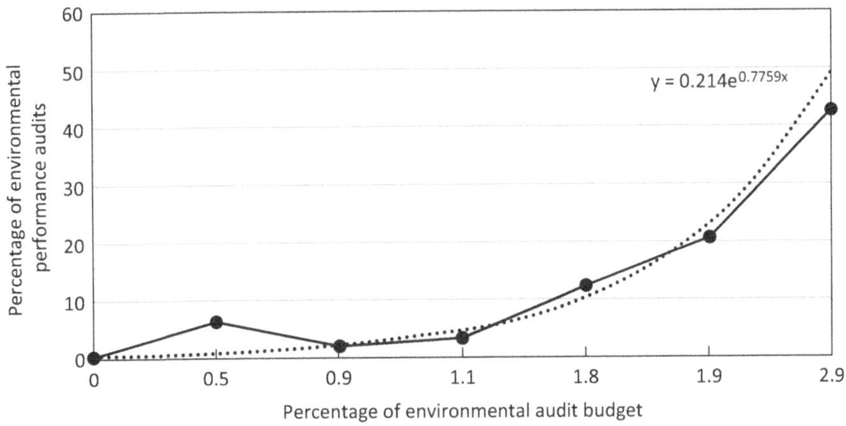

Figure 6.2 Relationship between budget (capacity) and environmental performance audit output.

Source: after Prasad, 2018.

performance audit output (Figure 6.2). As the percentage of their environmental audit budget increases, there is a proportionally greater increase in SAIs' output of environmental performance audits. This is consistent with expectations as environmental performance audit requires more resources. More environmental audit budget allocation, thus, should result in more environmental performance audits. However, the budgetary effect is non-linear, which is also confirmed by an analysis of data from a different source (the survey reported in Chapter 4). This suggests some sort of feedback loop causing this multiplier effect. The increased SAI budget may enhance SAI capacity in more than one way. For example, it may provide for additional staff, their training and capacity building, data collection, physical resources such as computer, internet and software packages, exchange of information and knowledge sharing through cooperation with other SAIs. These multiple benefits more likely create manifold increase in effective capacity; hence enhanced SAI environmental audit budget creates a non-linear increase in the output of environmental performance audit output.

Resources for environmental auditing

In about half of SAIs, 1–4 per cent of auditors work on environmental audits; in about one-sixth of SAIs, 5–9 per cent of auditors work on environmental audits; and in less than 10 per cent of SAIs, more than 10 per cent of auditors work on environmental audits (Table 6.4). About 35–40 per cent of SAIs reported in the 2009 and 2012 WGEA surveys having a separate department working on

Table 6.4 Environmental auditing resources (response percentage of SAIs in WGEA surveys)

Data item	*2009 (N = 106)*	*2012 (N = 112)*	*Average*
1. Percentage of employees working full- or part-time on environmental audits			
0%	9	22	16
1–4%	54	50	52
5–9%	19	13	16
Greater than 10%	9	8	9
N/A	9	7	8
2. Specific environmental audit department	40	35	38
3. Change in the share of environmental auditors			
Decreased	7	4	6
Remained same	58	66	62
Increased	33	29	31
N/A	2	1	2

Source: WGEA.

environmental auditing. A similar proportion (35 per cent) reported having a separate environmental department in the 2006 survey (WGEA, 2007: 28). About 50 per cent of SAIs conduct environmental audits along with other audits (i.e. auditors work part-time on environmental audits) while 40 per cent of them have auditors devoted full-time to environmental audits (WGEA, 2012a: 26). This is consistent with data on separate environmental auditing units in Table 6.4. The data in Table 6.4 suggest that while environmental auditing may be a small proportion of the overall activities of the SAIs, it is now a well- recognized discipline and resources allocated to it are either stable or increasing, but certainly not decreasing in the vast majority of SAIs.

Sufficiency of skills base

An overwhelming majority (close to 80 per cent) of SAIs (73 per cent developing and 88 per cent developed) consider that their skill base is sufficient to undertake environmental performance audits in the short-term (Figure 6.3). Further, a large majority (about 70 per cent) of SAIs also consider that their skill base is sufficient in the medium- to long-term. However, in the same survey, a majority (60 per cent) of SAIs identify insufficiency of resources as a constraint in undertaking more environmental performance audits. Prima facie, these two do not seem to be consistent. In this regard, it may be noted, however, that skills (or human resources) is not the only resource required for audit. Financial resources

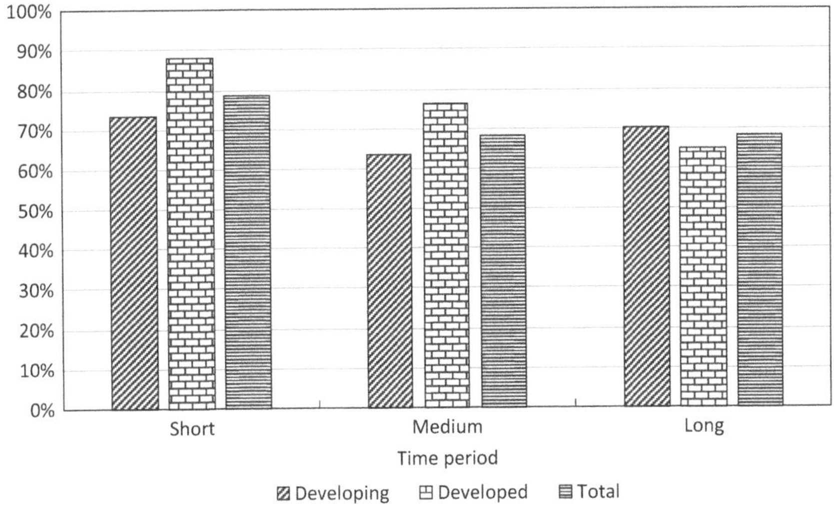

Figure 6.3 Do you consider your SAI's skill base sufficient to undertake environmental performance audit in (1) short-term (1–3 years); (2) medium-term (3–5 years); and (3) long-term (5–10 years)? 'Yes' response (percentage) – developing SAIs (*N* = 30); developed SAIs (*N* = 17); total SAIs (*N* = 47). The original responses were weighted as follows: (a) Yes – 1; (b) no and N/A – 0.

including infrastructure are also a major input to performance audits. Even if human resources exist (assuming funds are available to pay salaries), if there is not sufficient operating budget (such as for travel, communication, equipment, stationery and publication costs) available, it will not be easy to undertake performance audits. Additionally, an SAI's priority is also a key consideration in undertaking more environmental audits in the long term. In the overall scheme of things, the environment may not be a high priority. One SAIs notes that resource constraint 'is common to all matters, not only regarding to environmental matters'. Another SAI echoes this sentiment:

> [R]esources do act as a constraint for all our audit work, including performance audits of environmental policies and programs. [However, it is not], an undue constraint on audits of environmental policies and programs specifically, given that we cover the whole of government.

One SAI makes an apt observation that 'environmental topics compete with other topics for attention on our work program'. Though made by a developed SAI, this observation applies to all SAIs without a specific environmental audit mandate and consequently has implications for environmental auditing particularly in developing countries. A developing country SAI notes: 'environmental issues are not a big priority in most developing countries. More efforts are made to auditing financial issues of programs.'

Skills augmentation in specific disciplines

Notwithstanding sufficiency of their in-house skills base, about two-thirds of SAIs (82 per cent developing and 39 per cent developed country SAIs) consider it desirable to have in-house skills in some specific discipline related to environment performance audits. Environmental economics, geographical information system (GIS), ecology, nature protection and climate change are the most sought-after specific disciplines. Some reasons for the stark contrast between developed and developing country SAIs may be that: (1) developed SAIs already have specific in-house skills; (2) developed SAIs may prefer to hire a consultant than augment skills in-house; and (3) developed SAI do not consider that there is a need for skill augmentation in any specific discipline related to environment performance audits. Compared with the developing SAIs (that still have considerable emphasis on actual results), the developed SAIs place more emphasis on systems and processes. Therefore, the latter may not consider it necessary or desirable to have, or augment, skills in specific disciplines related to environment performance audits. For them, skill/knowledge in generic areas such as government processes and accountability framework and programme governance is adequate to assess performance of programmes. A developed SAI notes that 'in most cases, a detailed technical knowledge of environmental matters is not necessary to undertake a performance audit on environmental topics' as the government often is a 'financier' rather than executor of such 'specialist' activities. This is an interesting observation that not only describes aptly the environmental management situation in many developed countries, but also raises some fundamental issues about SAIs' role, and the skill set they need for auditing performance in a situation of devolved programme governance, including, for instance, the delivery of public services by the private sector, either wholly or partly in partnership with government, commonly known as 'public–private partnership'. However, such matters need separate investigation that others are undertaking (see, for example, Barrett, 2011; English et al., 2010).

Data and information

Data form a critical component of evidence for performance auditing. It is rarely possible to get all information required for performance auditing, as data might be inadequate, inaccurate or conflicting (INTOSAI, 2004: 114). This is more so for environmental matters, where problems with data availability and credibility challenges are known to exist (see, for example, OCED, 1998: 16; Uitto, 2014).

Adequacy of data

Only one-fifth of SAIs indicate (Figure 6.4) that data related to environmental policies and programmes have 'mostly/always' been adequate to make conclusions about their performance; a large proportion (about two-fifths) of SAIs consider that data have 'very often' been adequate; about one-quarter say they have 'often'

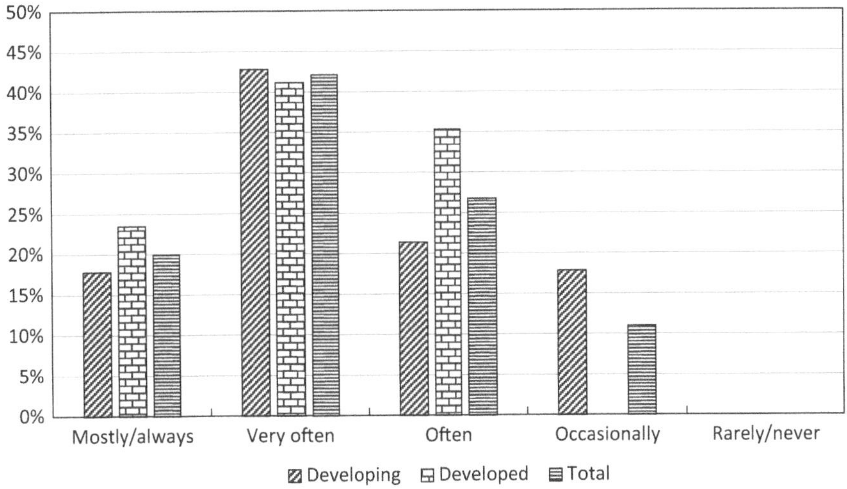

Figure 6.4 How often in the last five years have the data (other than financial data) related to environmental policies and programmes, either publicly available or sourced from auditees or other agencies, been adequate to make conclusions about their performance – (a) mostly/always (90 per cent or more of the time); (b) very often (50–89 per cent of the time); (c) often (30–49 per cent of the time); (d) occasionally (10–29 per cent of the time); and (e) rarely/never (less than 10 per cent of the time)? Response (percentage) – developing SAIs (*N* = 28); developed SAIs (*N* = 17); total SAIs (*N* = 45).

been adequate; and about one-tenth of SAIs say data have only 'occasionally' been adequate. It is notable that about 90 per cent of SAIs consider that data have 'often' to 'always' been adequate and no SAI considers they have 'never' been adequate.

Data collection requires resources. As such, developed countries are more likely to have better data than developing countries. Consistent with this expectation, more developed SAIs (24 per cent) than developing SAIs (18 per cent) report that data related to environmental policies and programmes have been 'mostly adequate'. Compared with developing SAIs (21 per cent), a higher proportion of developed SAIs (35 per cent) also report data being 'often adequate'. However, almost a similar proportion of developing (43 per cent) and developed (41 per cent) SAIs report data being 'very often' adequate. Overall, while all of the developed SAIs consider data as being 'mostly adequate' to 'often adequate'; only four-fifths of the developing SAIs do so (about one-fifth of them consider data being only 'occasionally adequate').

A majority of SAIs acknowledge either 'weaknesses in the availability of data'; or 'problems regarding reliability and quality of environmental data from official sources'; or the 'need for greater consistency of environmental data to compare like with like'. 'Often the audited entities do not collect [data] in an organized and systematic manner.' 'On many occasions, data is fragmented and not comprehensive. Moreover, there is limited information related to outcomes of environmental programs.' One SAI notes that 'record keeping is poor especially relating to scientific measures from both the operators of the systems that affect the environment and the regulators that are supposed to ensure that the operators are within the set standards'. Another SAI observes that 'data availability has been a problem because it is not the culture of record keeping in most government agencies (mostly the local government)'. Due to its poor quality, yet another SAI had 'to mine data from varied sources to provide audit assurance'. 'In almost all our reports on environmental audits, we have a series of findings and conclusions about unreliability and incompleteness of official environmental data', observes one SAI.

Some SAIs that consider data as usually available still note the need for improvements such as the following: (1) 'The storage systems need to improve as [d]ata is stored on paper and rarely kept on an electronic database.' (2) 'Problem is to select the useful ones and work them to get what you want.' (3) '[W]hile we have been able to draw conclusions about the achievement of audit objectives for environmental audits, on occasions, these conclusions identify a lack of adequate data or insufficient performance measures to make definitive findings on the extent to which environmental programs have achieved their objectives.' Of the SAIs that consider data collection as adequate, one reports of a data governance system that may be considered good practice. Writing about its National System for Environmental Monitoring managed by an environmental agency (EA), the SAI observes:

> The system provides information on the elements of the environment and factors affecting it, on which base analysis, assessments and forecasts are performed to support the activities of preserving and protecting the environment from harmful effects. All measurements and observations are carried out by the [EA] in common, unified methods for sampling and analysis in accordance with the procedures ensuring the quality of measurements and data. All [EA] laboratories are accredited under the BS EN ISO/IEC 17025 – General requirements for competence in testing and calibration. EA maintains databases at national and regional level. Databases at national and regional level are structured in components of the environment and using common nomenclatures. The results from the monitoring and the managed public registers are available on the internet site of the [EA].

Based upon this monitoring, different environment-related ministries and departments publish 'reports, projects, analyses with information about indicators for the environmental status' on their websites, adds the SAI.

Measures taken in case of inadequacy of data

To overcome data inadequacy, about 60 per cent of SAIs have taken one, or all, of the following three measures: (1) asked the audited body to collect/generate data; (2) collected or generated data on their own; and (3) reported that data held by the audited body have not been adequate. However, the third option (62 per cent) has been taken by more SAIs than the previous two options (58 per cent). More than one-third of the SAIs either: (1) collected data with external assistance; or (2) agreed with stakeholders to use the available data. The greater emphasis on reporting of the inadequacy of data underlines the emphasis on transparency of the audit process. Further, as this recognizes the problem and brings it into the public domain, it is also likely to result in improved data collection efforts by auditees.

Except for reporting on the inadequacy of data, a higher proportion of the developing SAIs than the developed SAIs took some, or all, of the above measures to gather sufficient information for conclusions. The largest difference in this regard between the developing and developed SAIs' endeavours is for: (1) collecting data on their own (32 per cent); followed by (2) asking auditees to collect data (22 per cent); and (3) collecting data with external assistance (16 per cent). There is no difference between the developing and developed SAIs in agreeing with the stakeholders to use the available data. On the other hand, 20 per cent more developed SAIs than the developing SAIs report the inadequacy of data. This may suggest that developed SAIs are perhaps taking a more pragmatic view of the matter (i.e. letting the problem be recognized and solved by others) than the developing SAIs, who are trying to solve the data problem on their own.

Issues in the assessment of effectiveness of environmental policies and programmes

SAIs acknowledge that 'while impacts [of policies] may be qualitative or quantitative', due to their 'long-term effects' they are 'difficult to determine'. Difficulties are acknowledged in both measuring the environmental outcomes and attributing them to specific policies. 'Most of times the environmental policy's outcomes are hard to measure or even identify; and when you identify an outcome, [it] is harder to evaluate the weight of the environmental policy to achieve it.' Assessing the 'long term effectiveness of environmental policies is difficult because of many assumptions upon which outcomes were planned [that can] change by the end of planned period' – for example, 'climate change programs [are] challenging to assess [their] effectiveness', as it is not certain how the audited output 'will accumulate to make the intended long-term outcome'. Further, attribution of outcome to a policy is not certain, as one SAI notes that 'reduction in greenhouse gas emissions meets its commitments under the [United Nations Framework Convention on Climate Change] UNFCCC', but it is not clear 'to what extent is this the result of the climate change policies put in place, rather than the side effects of the economic crisis that started in 2009'. Another example cited is the audit of implementing groundwater policies, where it may 'take 20 to 100 years before the effects of policies on the status of groundwater' are visible.

Some SAIs consider that many 'programmes and policies are not designed according to the country's environmental, economic and social realities'. Consequently, they are 'without clear objectives; have neither institutions to fulfil their mandate, nor, have a specific timeframe for implementation'. Some 'policies are not clear to [even] auditees'. To overcome the difficulties in assessment related to the vagueness and 'long-term nature of environmental policies', some SAIs suggest 'interim' or 'intermediate' performance measures to assess their 'partial fulfilment'. For example, one SAI notes that,

> in the cases where programs have long-term outcomes, audited agencies should also develop intermediate output and outcome KPIs or explore the use of proxy measures that are measurable in the short to medium term that would give stakeholders confidence that the audited agency is on the path to achieving the long-term outcomes.

Major policy issues highlighted by environmental performance audits

The observations by two SAIs broadly capture the issues raised by SAIs generally. One SAI observed:

> the major issues highlighted by our environmental performance audits are: (a) the lack of developing of policies framework due to unclear mandate, role and jurisdiction issues of various stakeholders; (b) programs and plans are not supported with legal and administrative back-up; (c) the lack of formally approved policies; and (d) strategic and operational planning relating to various environmental initiatives was not always appropriate.

Another SAI noted,

> common issues include: the lack of sufficient performance measures and [key performance indicators] KPIs; lack of performance benchmarking at the start of the environmental programs; insufficient data retained to demonstrate the achievement of environmental performance; substandard information management and record-keeping; and insufficient monitoring of program performance by audited agency senior management.

The major policy issues identified by SAIs' environmental performance audits could be categorized in the following groups:

- Institutional: (1) overlapping mandates/lack of ownership; and (2) lack of coordination between related agencies and policies.
- Strategic, legal and conceptual: (3) lack of clear or executable policies; (4) lack of mainstreaming of environmental matters; tension between economic growth and environment; lack of strategic planning; (5) lack of performance measures or indicators.
- System and operational: (6) lack of information system; (7) lack of data; (8) lack of monitoring and evaluation; (9) inadequate compliance and enforcement.

- Resources: (10) lack of resource allocation to the environmental policies and programmes by the government.

It is noted that all these issues feature in the top ten issues identified in a survey by the WGEA (2012b: 13–14).

Lessons SAIs learned through environmental performance audits

SAIs' key observations in the survey undertaken for this study include the following: (1) 'Most problems come from lack of governance, coordination, integration, planning, monitoring, assessment.' (2) 'It is mostly a challenge for the implementers to meet the requirements of the policies.' (3) '[While] auditees are not eager to make major changes in systems immediately, if the quality of the audit is high and recommendations acceptable, the changes can be made.' (4) 'External point of view is very important for the environmental policy managers'; they appreciate when audits identify the 'core questions of their problems.'

Most other SAIs in the survey noted direct lessons that are broadly reflected by the following observations:

1 Environmental auditing is a very complex issue; it mostly includes more auditees; it is mostly cross-sectoral. The help from external experts is appreciated because of its complexity.
2 Plan realistic audits with clearly defined scope – don't be too ambitious. Discuss and agree audit criteria with the auditee. Produce audits that will be relevant and of interest to policy makers and other stakeholders. Be ready to experiment with different audit methodologies and obtain mutually supporting evidence from different sources. Do not underestimate the time needed to consult with experts, or overestimate their potential use. Environmental issues, and audit reports, should be seen in the context of overall sustainability – so economic and social issues also need to be considered when planning audits.
3 Constant validation of audit criteria and findings [at] technical levels of the auditee principal and expert interdisciplinary teams are key to the quality of reports. Developing good planning facilitates the implementation phase of the audit. Stakeholders should be taken into account. Using clear and quantifiable indicators within the audit criteria.
4 Avoid scientific debate (do not choose areas with clear lack of scientific agreement). Share experiences between SAIs to get new ideas for the audit approach. When drafting recommendations, one should think about the possible impact.
5 Communication with auditees, scholars, civil society and other actors is of great help; sharing experiences among SAIs is also helpful; and care has to be taken on how sample assessment results are understood.

In recognition of a long gestation period to detect impacts of some environmental policies, one SAI felt the need for 'sequential' (a series of) performance audits.

Overall, consistent messages emerging from the views of the SAIs on the matter are related to:

1 complexity of environmental auditing issues and related data limitations calling for well thought-out audit planning, clear scoping and defining of audit criteria;
2 avoidance of scientific debate, underestimation of time and overestimation of impact;
3 need for capacity building in specialist knowledge, skills/expertise;
4 need for a consultative approach with auditees and other stakeholders;
5 need for better communication of audit findings; and
6 need for sharing of experience through international cooperation including through joint/cooperative audits.

Matters to be specified in environmental policies to assess their performance

SAIs suggest that environmental policies and programmes should have clear objectives and targets and specify adequate, realistic and fair measures or indicators of performance to enable assessment of their performance. In most of the cases there are only process indicators, not outcome indicators. A combination of outcomes-based, outputs-based, activity-based and inputs-based key performance indicators (KPIs) or measures are considered appropriate to audit performance. While only a few SAIs cite the use of indicators indicating their unavailability, all of them consider their use desirable. The following two comments capture the essence of the points raised by the SAIs on the matters that should ideally be specified in environmental policies and programmes to facilitate assessment of their performance.

1 Environmental policies, as with other public policies, should have RACER indicators (Relevant, Acceptable, Credible, Easy, Robust). The policies should be translated into clearly defined actions whose execution can be managed and measured (whether these actions are 'stand alone' or integrated into other public policies). Responsibilities and funding for the actions should be clearly established. Coordination between stakeholders (public and private) is vital, given the cross-cutting nature of environmental policies – economic and social issues are usually also involved. Environmental policies and programmes must be integrated into other public policy areas, especially those higher-profile policies which may receive more direct public funding. There should be a long-term, though evolving, strategy so that sustainability and environmental issues can be addressed in a coherent way. There should be a well thought-out, though not necessarily complex, reporting system that includes procedures to check the accuracy/completeness of underlying data.

2 When elaborating policies and programmes, indicators for assessment of their performance should be clearly defined. Distinguishing between indicators for output/performed activity, for result and for impact is a pre-condition for carrying out effective monitoring during their implementation, assessment of the benefits and the effect for the society. The inclusion of interim indicators is a necessary condition to trace the progress of the different stages of programme implementation, thus ensuring opportunity for timely identification of problems and taking concrete and appropriate management decisions.

Conclusion

Key barriers to environmental performance auditing include: lack of skills or expertise within the SAI; insufficient data on the state of the environment; and insufficient monitoring and reporting systems. Key challenges confronting environmental performance auditing relate to: (a) deficient environmental policy formulation, and data and monitoring difficulties (governments responsible); (b) SAIs' mandate and resources (governments responsible); and (c) audit relationships and communication matters (SAIs responsible). SAIs identify major issues with environmental policies at several levels – institutional, strategic, operational and resource allocation. Complexity of environmental auditing issues requires (1) well thought-out audit planning, clear scoping and defining of audit criteria; (2) avoidance of scientific debate, underestimation of time and overestimation of impact; (3) need for capacity building in specialist knowledge and skills/expertise; (4) need for a consultative approach with auditees and other stakeholders; (5) need for better communication of audit findings; and (6) need for sharing of experience through international cooperation, including through joint/cooperative audits.

Notes

1 INTOSAI has seven regional groups: OLACEFS, AFROSAI, ARABOSAI, ASOSAI, PASAI, CAROSAI and EUROSAI. See Chapter 2 for further details.

2 WGEA surveys categorize the USA and Canada responses together as belonging to the 'Other' region. Therefore a 100 per cent 'yes' response to any question means they have both responded with 'yes' and a 50% 'yes' response mean that one of them has not responded with 'yes'.

References

Barrett, P. (2011). Commentary: performance audit of PPPs – getting the basics right. *Australian Accounting Review*, 21(1), 99–106.

English, L. M., Guthrie, J., Broadbent, J. & Laughlin, R. (2010). Performance audit of the operational stage of long-term partnerships for the private sector provision of public services. *Australian Accounting Review*, 20(1), 64–75.

INTOSAI. (2004). *Performance Audit Guidelines: ISSAI 3000–3100*. Stockholm: INTOSAI.

INTOSAI. (2012). Environmental auditing: current and future challenges. *International Journal of Government Auditing*, 39(3), 21–22.

OECD. (1998). *OECD Environmental Performance Reviews: Australia*. Paris: OECD.

Prasad, A. (2016). *Environmental Performance Auditing by Supreme Audit Institutions: Progress, Practice and Prospects*. PhD thesis, The Australian National University, Canberra. Retrieved 15 April 2017 from http://hdl.handle.net/1885/112881

Prasad, A. (2018). Global trends in performance auditing of environmental policies and programs. implementation. *Journal of Sustainability Science and Management*. In press.

Uitto, J. I. (2014). Evaluating environment and development: lessons from international cooperation. *Evaluation*, 20(1), 44–57.

Van Leeuwen, S. (2004). Developments in environmental auditing by supreme audit institutions. *Environmental Management*, 33(2), 163–172.

WGEA. (2007). *Fifth Survey on Environmental Auditing*. Stockholm: INTOSAI.

WGEA. (2009). *Sixth Survey on Environmental Auditing*. Stockholm: INTOSAI.

WGEA. (2012a). *Seventh Survey on Environmental Auditing*. Stockholm: INTOSAI.

WGEA. (2012b). *Improving National Performance: Environmental Auditing Supports Better Governance and Management*: Stockholm: INTOSAI.

Yusoff, H. N. (2013). Understanding environmental audit in the public sector: Malaysian perspective. *Jurnal Teknologi*, 62(1), 25–30.

7 Perspectives and prospects

Environmental performance auditing has all the characteristics and challenges of performance auditing generally. However, there are several challenges specific to environmental auditing (INTOSAI, 2012). This final chapter draws together perspectives from earlier chapters on trends, current practices and issues and challenges in environmental performance auditing and considers their prospects into the future.

What have been the trends in environmental performance auditing?

Key findings from trend analysis of the two decades 1992–2012 of environmental performance audits include the following:

1. Environmental performance audits have been growing in number and possibly in complexity. Increasingly more Supreme Audit Institutions (SAIs) have been undertaking such audits. However, the growth in environmental performance audits has been uneven. About half of the environmental performance audits over these two decades have been produced by ten countries. About half of SAIs (largely concentrated in Africa and the Caribbean) did not produce any environmental performance audits during this period, suggesting capacity gaps.[1]
2. There is a link between global economic conditions and global output of environmental performance audits. As global GDP has steadily increased, so has the output of environmental performance audits. Further, transient fluctuations in global economic conditions are also reflected in the variable global output of environmental performance audits.
3. There is also a link between the broader economic conditions of the parent country of SAIs and their output of environmental performance audits – developed country SAIs as a group, though smaller in number, have produced more environmental performance audits than developing country SAIs. Due to their sheer numbers, overall, developing country SAIs seem to be gradually overtaking developed country SAIs in the production of environmental performance audits. However, as the former are also more vulnerable to any downturn in broader economic conditions, such as the global financial crisis

(GFC), these have more pronounced effects on the output of environmental performance audits of developing country SAIs than developed country SAIs.

4 The economic development conditions of the parent country of SAIs also determine environmental topics they audit. Development and sustenance issues (e.g. drinking water, agriculture) are more important to developing country SAIs. Life quality issues, such as climate change and governance, are more important to developed country SAIs. As would be expected, SAIs, being part of the wider society of their countries, reflect wider societal priorities in their audit work.

5 There is a strong correlation between membership of the Working Group on Environmental Auditing (WGEA) and the output of environmental performance audits. WGEA-member SAIs have produced more environmental performance audits than the SAIs that are not members of the WGEA. Among the WGEA members, developing country SAIs outperform their developed peers in producing environmental performance audits. However, among the non-members, in contrast, developed SAIs have produced more environmental performance audits than their developing peers. This underscores the importance of environmental awareness (reflected via WGEA membership) vis-à-vis economic factors.

How is environmental performance auditing currently practised?

Key findings from the survey of SAIs are that current practice in environmental performance auditing includes the following:

1 Environmental matters are now part of the mainstream of performance auditing as an overwhelming majority of SAIs consider them in their strategic audit planning.

2 Irrespective of the existence of a specific mandate for environmental auditing, SAIs predominantly use a structured approach to topic selection that includes, among others, risk assessment, materiality and salience. As environmental topics compete with other topics, such as those related to health and education, for the attention of SAIs (with a non-specific mandate for environmental audit), this method disadvantages environmental performance auditing especially in developing countries, where environmental issues may not be a high priority. SAIs without a specific mandate for environmental auditing also use a sectoral approach to topic selection, in which environmental matters are selected as per their relative importance. Like other topics, environmental matters are also selected as a consequence of requests from stakeholders. Overall, however, environmental performance audit work is a significant, but still small, proportion of the total performance audit work of SAIs.

3 The majority of SAIs (proportionally more developing than developed SAIs) develop criteria for environmental performance audits in consultation with auditees. Predominantly, SAIs (proportionally more developed than

developing SAIs) explicitly specify the criteria for environmental performance audit. Likewise, SAIs (more developed than developing SAIs) predominantly derive criteria for environmental performance audits from official sources, such as relevant policies and auditees' performance indicators. However, SAIs are highly sceptical of the reliability of official sources of information.

4 Almost all SAIs use some standards or guidelines for quality assurance of their environmental performance audits.
5 SAIs use about 15 different types of methods to collect evidence for performance audits. The five most popular methods of evidence collection, in order, are: document examination; officials' interview; site visit; literature survey; and system/process review. On average, developed SAIs seem to be using more methods than developing SAIs. Key factors considered in the decision of methods to use include: the complexity of the topic; objectives and scope of the audit; and availability of resources – both financial and non-financial, including human resources.
6 SAIs overwhelmingly (more developing than developed) consider that cooperation with other SAIs, directly or indirectly, via the WGEA has benefited them by improving their understanding of environmental matters; improving skills of staff; and raising the profile of environmental performance auditing generally. Further, SAIs also overwhelmingly consider that cooperative audits that WGEA promotes lead to better audit quality and more international environmental cooperation.

The comparative study of three countries (Australia, Canada and India) shows how local institutional settings, culture and traditions can impact the practise of performance audits. While there are broad similarities between the three countries' SAIs' audit practices (e.g. selection of topics, overall conduct of audit, use of standards and reporting to parliament), there are also significant differences between them. For example, the SAI of India can audit all levels of government. Therefore, there is a great variety in its reports in terms of format, content and size. On the other hand, even though Australia and Canada are socio-economically similar, the Canadian SAI is far ahead of its Australian counterpart in terms of the volume of environmental performance audits. This is attributed to the special environmental mandate of the Canadian SAI. Even adhering to the same basic principle that a performance audit must conclude against audit objectives, the three SAIs widely vary in their approach to this matter. The Canadian performance audit conclusions are very closely aligned to the audit objectives, whereas conclusions of the Indian audit reports are not well aligned. The alignment between audit objectives and conclusions of the Australian audit reports are somewhere in between. Undoubtedly, as SAIs serve their parliament, their reporting style and preferences would have evolved to better suit that requirement. Despite being rooted in the same basic tenets of democracy, no two parliaments are identical in their characteristics. Likewise, it would be expected that no two SAIs would be identical in their performance auditing practice.

Having said that, it appears that the difference in reporting styles of SAIs – especially the difference between different reports of the same SAI – is technical in nature and is a consequence of: (1) non-adherence to their existing standards perhaps due to deficient quality control; and (2) an absence of general attention to performance audit reporting. SAIs individually need to tighten adherence to their own standards. Further, they need to work together via the International Organization of Supreme Audit Institutions (INTOSAI) to enhance the quality of performance audit reporting.

What are the key issues and challenges in environmental performance auditing?

Broadly, these issues are of three types: (1) relating to environmental policies that are within the realm of governments; (2) relating to SAIs but mostly within the realm of governments, such as mandate and resources; and (3) relating to SAIs that need to be addressed by themselves, such as communication and relationship matters.

Environmental policy design and data

Environmental policy-related issues within the realm of governments include: (1) overlapping mandates; (2) lack of coordination between related agencies and policies; (3) lack of clear or executable policies; (4) lack of mainstreaming of environmental matters; (5) lack of information systems; (6) lack of monitoring and evaluation, including a lack of data and performance measures or indicators; (7) inadequate compliance and enforcement; and (8) lack of resource allocation to the environmental policies and programmes by the government. Notwithstanding the challenges of environmental data (van Dijk et al., 2014), some guidance, resources and methods are available (see WGEA, 2013a) that SAIs can use when high-quality environmental data are lacking. Further, social networking tools such as LinkedIn and Facebook that are already being used to monitor environmental issues by some governmental and non-governmental organizations present new opportunities as well as challenges for SAIs (WGEA, 2013a: 44). A related issue is the long-term nature of some environmental programmes and policies. Developing some interim or intermediate performance measures is considered a possible solution (see, for example, Barrett, 2012; Barrett, 2015). Some SAIs suggest in the survey for this study that a combination of outcomes-based, outputs-based, activity-based and input-based key performance indicators that are relevant, acceptable, credible, easy and robust should ideally be specified in the environmental policies and programmes to facilitate their performance audit.

Mandate

Mandate is the primary enabler that determines what types of audit SAIs can undertake and whom they can audit. The overwhelming majority of SAIs do have a performance audit mandate, and nearly all of them have access to the national government. However, only two-thirds of SAIs have access to state/provincial and local governments and to government undertakings, while fewer than half of them have access to semi-government bodies. Access to non-government public and private organizations is extremely limited. In the modern policy environment, when more and more governmental programmes – including environmental programmes – are delivered in partnership between several governments, and/or between the public, private and community sectors, performance auditing faces significant challenges due to the model of SAIs' existing mandate. A complementary model of performance auditing is required in which audit offices at different levels of government, and for that matter SAIs and private sector auditors, can work together to audit the performance of environmental initiatives funded and executed by several governments and even by the private sector. While a specific environmental audit mandate is not necessary, it does drive performance auditing of environmental issues. While governments could reconsider mandates of SAIs to better serve the needs of the future, until such a time as that happens, SAIs will need to innovate to better utilize their exiting mandates to audit under the emerging circumstances.

Skills and resources

In addition to their mandates, SAIs need adequate resources/capacity to undertake audits. The highest concentration of SAIs that have not undertaken any environmental performance audits is in Africa – a region of lower economic development. This suggests a lack of capacity in SAIs to undertake performance audits generally and environmental performance audits particularly. Skill/capacity deficiencies in Africa and other regions should be a matter of concern for governments, INTOSAI and donor agencies, such as the World Bank, International Monetary Fund, the Asian Development Bank, UNDP, UNEP and even the individual donor nations, given that these regions or individual countries will also be receiving developmental assistance as part of the new sustainable development agreement (see, for example, UN, 2015: paragraphs 28, 43). The donor agencies and nations should invest in capacity development of these SAIs, especially in the developing country SAIs that have not been able to undertake environmental performance audits. The INTOSAI Development Initiative (IDI), along with donor agencies, has been working on this capacity development, but significantly more is required. As performance auditing is profoundly affected by local factors, capacity building should be tailored and targeted towards individual countries.

For the SAIs that have undertaken environmental performance audits, there is a non-linear relationship between SAIs' budget and output of environmental performance audits. An increase in an SAI's budget produces a non-linear positive effect on environmental performance auditing due to simultaneous multiple effects that reinforce each other, such as enhancement of skill/capacity, availability of equipment and resources for cooperation. While SAIs indicate that their current skill/capacity is sufficient to undertake environmental performance audits (Chapter 4), two key issues should be noted in forming a view of the sufficiency of skills across SAIs. (1) The survey only represents the views of the SAIs that are already undertaking environmental performance auditing; there are about 100 SAIs that are not undertaking such audits, likely due in part to inadequate skills. (2) Skills seem to be sufficient only in the context of short-term work – topics chosen for audit. If SAIs do not have skills in certain areas, they may not choose such topics for audit. For their long-term requirements, SAIs do indicate a need or desire for development of skills in certain areas – for example in environmental economics. Further, due to emerging challenges (e.g. sustainable development), there will continue to be a need for skills development to undertake environmental audits. For example, SAIs will need to develop sustainability reporting frameworks for the public sector, and subsequently provide assurance on sustainability reporting when it is introduced (WGEA, 2013b: 36). To meet the growing need for specialist training in environmental auditing, WGEA, in partnership with the SAI of India, has established a global training facility – the International Centre for Environmental Audit and Sustainable Development (iCED) in Jaipur, India (Prasad, 2012). Starting in 2013, iCED has been delivering training courses to the staff of various SAIs. However, participation in the iCED training courses will likely be determined by the availability of financial support, as the majority of SAIs that are willing to participate may not have the financial means to do so (WGEA, 2012a: 71). It goes without saying that financial resources are as important as human resource (skills) for undertaking performance audits. A large majority of SAIs in the survey (see Chapter 4) indicate that insufficient resources are a constraint to undertaking more environmental performance audits.

Strengthening SAIs' capacity is critical to enhancing the accountability of government administration that is instrumental in implementing the sustainable development agenda. Two UN resolutions in quick succession (A/66/209 of December 2011 and A/C.2/69/L.25/Rev1 of November 2014) have called for action on this. Consequently, all governments should strengthen their SAI to enable the achievement of post-2015 sustainable development goals. However, having more resources would not automatically translate into more capacity and skills. SAIs will need to proactively develop skills and capacities in areas of identified needs. For example, environmental economics and GIS are two such areas in which many SAIs consider a need for capacity development.

Communication

Performance audits have led to significant improvements in the governance of environmental policies as well as in the performance of environmental policies and programmes (Prasad, 2016: 108). However, there is considerable scope to improve impacts by actions on the part of SAIs. Reed and Cinq-Mars (2014) identify some practical measures for increasing the impact of environmental performance audits. These include: (1) selecting topics of interest to the public and to parliament; (2) focusing on results in audit objectives; (3) going beyond compliance in audit criteria; (4) timing of audits to 'pivot points' in the environmental issues cycle, such as periodic review of key environmental legislation/programmes; (5) when scoping audits, consider linkages between issues by doing multiple audits on one topic over years; (6) and when determining focus consider drivers of environmental degradation. Further, SAIs can enhance impacts of their audits by improving their communication with auditees, parliament and the public. Improving communication and engagement with auditees perhaps is still 'low hanging fruit' with huge potential to enhance audit impacts. Notwithstanding this, unlike a law court, however, SAIs do not have enforcement powers to ensure implementation of their recommendations by government. In this respect, they depend primarily on parliament as the ultimate owner of policies and as the primary client of their audit reports. Therefore, they must proactively and responsively engage with their parliament to enhance the impact of their audits.

To increase impact, SAIs need to enhance the quality of reporting of their performance audits. Unlike the conduct of performance audits, there is no general standard for the content of performance audit reports (Suzuki, 2004). Consequently, the contents of performance audit reports not only vary between the SAIs, they also vary between different audit reports of the same SAI. As noted in Chapter 5, the most notable variation in the audit reports is the coverage of methodology. While a lack of interest among the parliamentarians – the primary client of SAIs – in methodological details (Lonsdale, 1999: 145–146; McPhee, Former Auditor General of Australia, personal communication) is acknowledged, it does not absolve the SAIs of their professional responsibility to maintain rigour in their reporting work. Description of audit criteria in performance audit reports is another area that requires attention. The deficiencies in the coverage of both methodology and criteria in performance audit reports point to a systemic antithesis of auditing that is to promote transparency and accountability. Performance audit reports are highly visible public documents that are used by a range of stakeholders including parliamentarians, governments, the media and the public for various purposes. Given their growing importance, they need some assurance on their contents. Concerted global action is warranted to enhance the quality of reporting of performance audits. For the SAIs that already have reporting standards, reviewing and implementing them rigorously is highly desirable.

Innovation in audit reporting is required to reach wider audiences. As different audiences have different needs, it may be challenging for SAIs to meet all such needs in one report. However, the advances in information and communication technologies can be harnessed by SAIs to meet this challenge, such as publishing different versions of the report (summary and full report) on the internet, and using social media such as Facebook and Twitter to reach different types of audiences. Some audit offices are already doing that. For example, the SAI of India uses small coloured booklets to communicate performance audit messages to clients. The booklets include a summary of key findings and conclusions, accompanied by colour photos and an electronic copy of the report on a CD-ROM. A peer review (Australia et al., 2012: 40) considers that this innovative way to reach a broader audience and draw attention to important community issues is a good practice. The SAI of Australia has started publishing a periodic newsletter, *Audit Focus*, capturing general lessons from its audit work – what works and what doesn't in public sector administration (ANAO, 2018). An SAI notes in the survey for this study (Chapter 4) that

> we are experimenting with alternative ways of presenting our work – using more interactive pdfs (portable document formats) rather than long-form reports. While this is not confined to our work on environmental issues, [this] is one of the areas where we are making more use of this new format than most.

'Ensuring publicity and transparency, wide media coverage of problems and difficulties in the environmental protection identified during audit work' is one of the lessons noted by SAIs in the survey (Chapter 4), which highlights the importance of communication. Recognizing the 'preponderance of stakeholders in the environmental domain', the audit offices should reach beyond the usual audiences to specialized media, academics, journals, civil society, grassroots organizations and today's youth to reinforce the messages and impact. This obviously requires a communication strategy beyond reports, 'news releases, news conferences and interview with the usual media' (Reed and Cinq-Mars, 2014).

Currently, SAIs' recommendations are buried in their performance audit reports. Sometimes SAIs undertake follow-up audits to assess how their recommendations are being implemented. Depending upon the politico-administrative arrangements, sometimes parliamentary committees also follow-up on the implementation of the SAIs' recommendations. However, the public is rarely made aware of the implementation of the recommendations. This, in some way, limits the benefits of public auditing that includes letting the public know how government/administration is responding to the recommendations for improvements. One way of realizing the hidden potential of public auditing is that SAIs put a database of their performance audit recommendations on their website, which is updated periodically to show the status of implementation. This may put the department(s)/minister(s) under more public scrutiny, as the public may question government directly, or via their member of parliament, as to why audit recommendations have not been implemented. As this will put the spotlight directly on the administration/government and is likely to cause some discomfort, some resistance is expected. However, given their independence and standing, SAIs can implement this through a careful, cautious but consultative approach.

In many countries – for example, Australia and the UK – SAIs recently have concluded that producing audit reports is not enough for effecting beneficial change (Lonsdale, 2011), so they have started producing better practice guides (BPGs) incorporating the learnings from their audits. While some government officials have welcomed them, asking for more of BPGs and less of audits (McPhee, 2011: 11), it is also considered as a conflict of interest and potential threat to independence because it is perceived as stepping outside the competence of SAIs

(Barrett, 2012). As a consequence, there has been some rethinking – for example, the SAI of Australia has decided to discontinue producing BPGs (Hehir, 2016).

Collaboration

The connectedness of the modern world means that SAIs cannot afford to work in isolation to preserve their independence. They need to come out of their insularity to collaboratively work with others, such as, civil society organizations (CSOs), non-government organizations (NGOs), universities and research organizations in the public and private sector, to make their audits more participatory and thus more accessible, relevant and beneficial to the wider society. The public audit is now also considered as a means of community empowerment and agent of social change (see, for example, Rubenstein, 2001; Stern, 2005). Performance audits, by bringing information that is otherwise hidden in government departments out into the public domain, can empower the community to raise questions about the performance of government programmes, thus making government more accountable. UN Resolution A/66/209 notes that citizens and civil society are as important as addressees of audit reports and recommendations as competent political bodies, and they also contribute to effective control through public debate. Bhandari (2014) cites several examples of various models of involvement of CSOs in public audits in India, Africa, the Philippines, Mexico and Korea.

While the involvement of CSOs and NGOs is a welcome sign, this also presents some risks to the SAIs that need to be managed. For example, confidentiality of information needs to be maintained. Further, many CSOs and NGOs are known to have views that some may consider partisan. In working with these organizations, SAIs need to be careful not to get involved in policy advocacy, lest it discredits their objectivity and independence – the core foundation of their reputation. This way, they could lose more influence than they would gain. Notwithstanding the risks involved, it is unlikely that SAIs would be able to operate effectively in isolation. In the modern era of exponentially growing connectivity enabled by the digital revolution, SAIs may perhaps struggle for influence if they do not transform themselves as connected organizations. They will need to make some strategic choices if they would like to be the source of authentic, objective and timely performance information that is enabled by partnership with others; or compete with so many other sources of information and risk fading into irrelevance, being perceived as obsolete. While they have a monopoly over government audit, this will only serve to the extent that the public at large see them as the source of timely, authentic and beneficial information. With limited resources and a lot to do, perhaps the question about engaging in partnerships may no longer be of 'if', but rather of 'how' they do it. What they use the partnerships for, rather than whom they partner with, will be a bigger determinant of their influence. If they concentrate on building partnerships and collaborations to gather data and information, develop analytical tools and methods, and develop and disseminate knowledge, SAIs are likely to gain more influence. There is a range of bodies that SAIs can collaborate with in these areas, such as universities, statistical and research bodies, NGOs, CSOs and think tanks.

SAIs also need to promote research to develop new tools and methods to enable auditing amid growing complexity of government business characterized by multilateralism, public–private partnerships, privatization and outsourcing. While WGEA has been undertaking significant research and has been producing guidance material, it is noted that most of this research has been undertaken by SAIs. While no doubt useful, it is considered that the WGEA research endeavour would benefit from participation by universities and other research bodies. SAIs are busy workplaces, generally challenged by a lack of adequate resources and mostly working to deadlines. This work environment of 'daily grind' is not very conducive to 'blue sky' thinking and detailed research that may be required to develop the audit methodologies of the future. For example, the research and development expertise of universities and research bodies could be tapped to develop environmental accounting and sustainability reporting and assurance. SAIs, through the WGEA or individually, could collaborate with universities to undertake such research. With cross-fertilization of ideas from SAIs and academics, such research could enrich the discipline of environmental performance auditing. Successful collaborations between professionals in government and outside in other professions, such as law, medicine and engineering, are worth emulating in performance auditing.

SAIs and universities are not well connected for several reasons, including SAIs' relatively lower budgetary implications for environmental performance auditing, lack of interest in universities and the usefulness of research produced by the universities (Prasad, 2016: 182). However, on the positive side, the evolving nature of environmental performance auditing is acknowledged and the need for research is recognized by SAIs. Some positive developments are already visible. For example, the SAIs of the USA and Uganda (on behalf of the WGEA), in addition to their SAI peers from several countries, worked with Columbia University and statistical offices/bureaus from a number of countries to produce preliminary guidance on 'Environmental Accounting' (WGEA, 2010). Likewise, the SAI of Finland, in addition to its SAI peers from several countries, worked with the University of Canterbury (UK), the Association of Chartered Certified Accountants (UK) and a Finnish private sector company, Tofuture, to produce WGEA (2013b) guidance on 'Sustainability Reporting'. This is a welcome sign and augers well for the future of environmental performance auditing.

Strengthening the WGEA

International cooperation with other SAIs has proved to be beneficial to capacity building and quality improvement of audits. The WGEA that has been promoting cooperation among SAIs on environmental auditing is showing early signs of stress. For example, the SAIs contacts on the WGEA website are not regularly updated and the publication of the 8th tri-annual survey was delayed – both suggesting capacity constraints in the WGEA. It is noted that the WGEA is currently an under-resourced (or unresourced) voluntary organization. Unlike its parent body (INTOSAI), the WGEA does not have a permanent secretariat and staff to manage its day-to-day operations. The secretariat support to the WGEA is provided on a voluntary basis by the Chair of the WGEA, which rotates among members. It should be noted that the secretariat manages a huge amount of data and information, in addition to providing administrative support to the WGEA. Due to a transient and under-resourced secretariat, there is a risk that valuable data and information held by the WGEA will become fragmented. It is understood, for example, that the data generated by the WGEA tri-annual surveys (eight so far) are not held in one location. Compared with its limited resources, demand on the WGEA is likely to increase in the future – for example, to produce guidance material on emerging issues. Further, in view of the adoption of new sustainable development goals, the WGEA will need to collaborate more with other international bodies such as the UNEP and UNDP.

In view of the above, there is a strong case for strengthening the WGEA to maintain and enhance the benefits it provides. This requires providing a permanent secretariat to the WGEA for its more effective functioning. This could result, among other things, in better collaboration, better management of valuable data and more value-added information products. For example, the current rudimentary WGEA database of environmental audit reports could be enhanced to periodically update the type of analysis produced in Chapter 3; more analysis of the WGEA tri-annual survey data could be made possible; and more value-added/tailor-made information products could be generated. These information products could be made available to governments and donor agencies – for example, to inform capacity-building efforts in SAIs. Further, a permanent secretariat could work on building better collaboration with other regional and international bodies such as the Asian Development Bank (ADB), the World Bank and UNEP. The UN, the World Bank, ADB and other financing/donor bodies may consider bearing the costs involved in strengthening the WGEA.

Limitations

The analyses reported in this book are inevitably constrained by the available data. For example, more environmental performance audits may exist than those available on the WGEA database that were analysed for the global trend analysis in Chapter 3. Some individual results may change if such hidden data were to be added to the analysis. While it is unlikely that this would lead to any large changes in the overall trends over the two decades studied, it would be valuable to extend the analysis with more data and to a longer period. It is considered that the three empirical analyses provide a sufficiently robust basis for this book. However, it is noted that later research or policy learning might extend this work through accessing more or finer-scale data. For example, another survey of SAIs may provide more insights into their current environmental performance auditing practices and challenges they face, and further case studies beyond the three countries investigated here, which would likely unearth some more issues with practice.

Future research

Several issues identified during this study warrant further academic attention:

1 Broader legal and conceptual challenges related to performance auditing amid dispersal of responsibilities at various levels – internationally between countries and domestically between various levels of government and between the public, private and community sectors.
2 Institutional cooperation/complementarity of SAIs and subnational audit offices on one hand and between audit offices and other accountability/integrity bodies and research agencies in the public and private sectors on the other.
3 Performance auditing by SAIs of government initiatives funded through international donations that lie outside national budgets.
4 Performance review by other (non-audit) public bodies.
5 Social audits and public participation in audits by SAIs, e.g. involvement of the general public and civil society organizations.
6 SAIs' research and development agenda generally, and particularly to meet the new sustainable development goals.
7 Impact of non-financial global events on environmental performance auditing, such as tri-annual meetings of INTOSAI and WGEA, adoption of the Millennium Development Goals in the early 2000s and negotiation of new multilateral environmental agreements.

As more data on environmental performance auditing becomes available in the future, it would be useful to further analyse the trend to investigate, among other things, whether the decline in environmental performance auditing post-2008 has reversed; and the continuous decline post-1996 in environmental performance auditing in low-income countries and reasons for that. This research could only broadly relate economic factors such as gross per capita national income and economic development level to environmental performance auditing through a univariate analysis. To further understand this relationship, more investigation, possibly through a multivariate correlation analysis, between pertinent socio-economic variables and environmental performance auditing is required. Annual expenditure on environmental policies and programmes is a good candidate variable to start with. Some other variables that may be considered include some socio-economic indices published by the World Bank, such as the Country Policy and Institutional Assessment (CPIA) index, International Development Association Resource Allocation Index (IRAI) and other relevant world development indices; and transparency in government (e.g. the Corruption Perception Index published by Transparency International). It is recognized that expenditure on environmental policies and programmes may not be easy to obtain for all countries. However, it might be possible to get it for some countries such as from the European Commission. It would be interesting to investigate, for those countries, if the environment sector is getting commensurate attention of SAIs in proportion to expenditure on the environment sector compared with other sectors, such as health and education. Further, future research: may benefit from interview with SAIs; investigate the environmental impact of environmental performance audits; and analyse environmental audit data differently, such as according to INTOSAI regional groups.

Further, it would be useful to investigate at about 2022–23 – the mid-term of the SDGs – how SAIs have operationalized the framework (including relevant indicators) currently under development (WGEA, 2017) for auditing the implementation of SDGs.

Actions to enable the effectiveness of implementation of SDGs

Environment and sustainable development issues are intrinsically linked. Therefore, SAIs' capacity to undertake environmental performance auditing can be an indicator of their capacity to monitor and enable the implementation of the 2030 Agenda for Sustainable Development (UN, 2015). As a positive sign, environmental performance auditing has been growing globally. However, significant challenges remain that require actions by governments (e.g. SAIs' mandate and budget, and design of relevant policies), donor agencies and SAIs. As concluding remarks, some actions are reiterated below that SAIs and INTOSAI can largely take themselves, without waiting for governments, to enhance their capacity to improve the effectiveness of implementation of policies and programmes aimed at achieving new sustainable development goals:

- INTOSAI, along with donor agencies, may particularly focus on building capacity in about half of SAIs – mostly in weaker economic regions such as Africa – that have not undertaken environmental performance audits, most likely due to capacity gaps.
- SAIs may consider enhancing their communication, their reporting standards and methods of reporting.
- SAIs may consider transforming themselves to work collaboratively with others for enhancing environmental performance auditing, including by developing new tools and methods for data collection and analysis.
- INTOSAI may consider strengthening the WGEA, for example by providing a permanent secretariat. INTOSAI may approach the UN, the World Bank, ADB and/or other financing/donor bodies for assistance to meet the costs involved in this endeavour.

Final remarks

This first systematic study of performance auditing of environmental policies and programmes undertaken by SAIs has investigated global trends, current practices and challenges therein. Environmental performance auditing is an evolving and challenging area of the old discipline of auditing. Aided by the WGEA, significant progress has been made, as demonstrated by the impressive growth in the global volume of environmental performance auditing. However, the progress has been uneven, primarily due to capacity gaps in SAIs, mostly from economically poor regions. Economic factors also influence the choice of audit topics and methods. Key challenges confronting environmental performance auditing relate to deficient environmental policy formulation and data and monitoring difficulties (governments responsible); SAIs' mandates and resources (governments responsible); and audit relationships and communication matters (SAIs responsible). Given the key role SAIs play in facilitating sustainable development, actions on all these fronts are necessary to meet the growing challenges of the future, including the attainment of the ambitious sustainable development goals by 2030.

Note

1 This finding is extended to 2016 by the SAIs response to the survey for this study. See note 1 in Chapter 4.

References

ANAO (2018). Audit focus. Retrieved 12 January 2018 from www.anao.gov.au/pubs/audit-focus

Australia (ANAO), Canada (OAG), Denmark (R), The Netherlands (AR) & United States of America (GAO). (2012). *International Peer Review of the Supreme Audit Institution of India*. New Delhi: Comptroller and Auditor General of India.

Barrett, P. (2012). Performance auditing: addressing real or perceived expectation gaps in the public sector. *Public Money and Management*, 32(2), 129–136.

Barrett, P. (2015b). Trust and confidence in government: whither public audit (unpublished).

Bhandari, C. K. (2014). Engaging civil service organizations in SAI audit *International Journal of Government Auditing*, 41(2), 24–29.

Hehir, G. (2016). Reflections on how far performance auditing has come from its roots in the 1970s to where we are today and where we are heading. Paper presented at the IMPACT-International Meeting of Performance Audit Critical Thinkers, 15–16 March 2016, Brisbane.

INTOSAI. (2012). Environmental auditing: current and future challenges. *International Journal of Government Auditing*, 39(3), 21–22.

Lonsdale, J. (1999a). Methods. In C. Pollitt, X. Girre, J. Lonsdale, R. Mul & H. Summa (Eds.), *Performance or Compliance? Performance Audit and Public Management in Five Countries* (pp. 125–148). Oxford: Oxford University Press.

Lonsdale, J. (2011). Introduction. In J. Lonsdale, P. Wilkins and T. Ling (Eds), *Performance Auditing: Contributing to Accountability in Democratic Government* (pp. 1–21). Cheltenham: Edward Elgar.

McPhee, I. (2011). The evolving role and mandate of the ANAO since federation. Paper presented at the Senate Occasional Lecture, Parliament House, Canberra. Retrieved 11 June 2014 from www.anao.gov.au/sites/g/files/net616/f/McPhee_Evolving_Role_and_Mandate_2011.pdf.

Prasad, N. (2012). New global training facility on environmental audit. *International Journal of Government Auditing*, 39(3), 16–17.

Prasad, A. (2016). *Environmental Performance Auditing by Supreme Audit Institutions: Progress, Practice and Prospects*. PhD thesis, The Australian National University, Canberra. Retrieved 15 April 2017 from http://hdl.handle.net/1885/112881

Reed, J. & Cinq-Mars, J. (2014). How to increase the impact of environmental performance audits. *International Journal of Government Auditing*, 41(2), 17–23.

Rubenstein, D. B. (2001). Audit as an agent of constructive consequence and social change. *Corporate Environmental Strategy*, 8(3), 234–241.

Stern, E. (2005). Auditing for social change in the context of the Millennium Development Goals. Paper presented at the 6th Global Forum on Reinventing Government Towards Participatory and Transparent Governance.

Suzuki, Y. (2004). Basic structure of government auditing by a supreme audit institution. *Government Auditing Review*, 11, 39–53.

UN. (2015). Transforming our world: the 2030 Agenda for Sustainable Development. Retrieved 15 March 2016 from https://sustainabledevelopment.un.org/content/documents/21252030%20Agenda%20for%20Sustainable%20Development%20web.pdf.

van Dijk, A., Mount, R., Gibbons, P., Vardon, M. & Canadell, P. (2014). Environmental reporting and accounting in Australia: progress, prospects and research priorities. Science of the Total Environment, 473, 338–349.

WGEA. (2010). *Environmental Accounting: Current Status and Options for SAIs*. Stockholm: INTOSAI.

WGEA. (2012a). *Seventh Survey on Environmental Auditing*. Stockholm: INTOSAI..

WGEA. (2013a). *Environmental Data: Resources and Options for Supreme Audit Institutions*. Stockholm: INTOSAI..

WGEA. (2013b). *Sustainability Reporting: Concepts, Frameworks and the Role of Supreme Audit Institutions*. Stockholm: INTOSAI..

WGEA. (2017). Message from the chair. *Greenlines*, 18(2). Retrieved 18 November 2017 from www.environmental-auditing.org/media/5317/eng17pu_green18n2sep.pdf.

Appendix: methods for evidence collection

Depending upon the need and available resources, various types of methods are used to collect evidence for performance auditing. Usually several methods are used together. These methods are described here to promote a common understanding.

Document examination: This involves reviewing documents such as files and records related to the relevant projects/programmes/activities of the auditees that may be in either paper or electronic form. This is the most commonly used methods for evidence collection (ANAO, 2015: 113). In a study of 105 water-related audits, the WGEA (2013: 53) reports that this method was used more than 95 per cent of the time.

Interview of officials: This involves conversations in the form of question-and-answer session(s) either face to face or over the phone. It may be structured (fact finding) or unstructured (exploratory). Sometimes short questions or clarifications may be sought through emails. Interview is also a widely used method for evidence collection. The WGEA (2013: 53) reports that this method was used in more than 90 per cent of audits.

Questionnaire/survey: A survey is the systematic collection of data usually from a large population by means of a questionnaire. Surveys may be conducted by various means such as post, telephone, internet and in-person. It is considered a cost-effective way (ANAO, 2015: 119) of collecting information that is usually not available in any other way (INTOSAI, 2004: 97). Caution is considered necessary in its use as surveys tend to have higher potential for errors and may be adversely affected by low response rates (WGEA, 2013: 56).

Stakeholders consultation (including survey): Consulting third parties, e.g. suppliers and customers, is a good means of collecting generally independent performance information about a government organization. While this may involve the methods already described (e.g. interview or survey), the approach has been considered as a separate method in this book. As SAIs assign different weights (often higher) to the information provided by customers/public and by the auditees themselves, it is considered that stakeholder consultation warrants a separate category. While the literature (e.g. INTOSAI, 2004; Lonsdale et al., 2011a; Pollitt et al., 1999; WGEA, 2013)) does not differentiate between the stakeholders and officials survey, it seems quite often that the word *survey* has been used in the context of stakeholder survey rather than in relation to the officials survey. If this interpretation is adopted, this method can also be considered as quite popular. About 35–40 per cent of audits in the WGEA study (2013: 56) used this method.

Site visit: Sometimes being called observation, direct observation or physical observation, this method involves directly watching or observing the objects, events or processes. Observing the physical condition of an asset (e.g. dam), and observing service delivery (e.g. sanitation) in a locality by the municipality are some examples. While considered very effective (WGEA, 2013: 54), the use of this method can potentially mask reality. For example, due to foreknowledge of a visit by the audit team on a particular day, a municipality might run a cleanliness drive to show the area as neat and clean, which it normally does not do. The WGEA (2013: 54) reports that this method was used in approximately 60 per cent of audits.

Sample examination: This involves examining a sample (limited number) of the population, for example checking a sample of transactions, inspecting a sample of beneficiary villages. This method is usually used in combination with other methods of evidence collection – for example, document examination or site visits. Samples may be statistically (random) or non-statistically (targeted) selected. Statistical samples are used to draw conclusion about the entire population, such as rate of compliance with a regulation, whereas non-statistical samples are used as examples of systemic issues (ANAO, 2015: 145). Statistical sampling is a discipline in itself in which the two most common methods used are simple random sampling and stratified random sampling. In random sampling, every member of the population has equal chance of selection, thus enabling an unbiased estimate. In stratified sampling the population is subdivided into groups, such as geographical regions or amount or type of transaction, and then samples are drawn randomly from within each group. It provides more reliable estimates than simple random sampling. However, it requires more effort in design and implementation and typically requires assistance of a statistician (ANAO, 2015: 150).

The sample examination method is used quite often. For example, Lonsdale (2011b: 100) reports a 30 per cent use of this method by NAO in its performance audits.

System/process review including database: This involves examination of subsystem(s) within an organization or programme/project/activity being audited – for example, a grant assessment process or a community consultation process. A complex information technology (IT) system such as a database used for storing and processing data – e.g., compliance with environmental approval conditions – is another example. This is used to investigate questions such as whether the system/process was designed and implemented in a fair, equitable and objective manner; how vulnerable the system process is to commission and omission errors; and whether appropriate control systems are in place. The method is widely used. For example, Lonsdale (2011b: 100) reports a 20 per cent use of the method in performance audits by NAO.

Expert opinion: This involves consulting people or organizations (outside the audit office) recognized for their skills, knowledge or experience in particular fields. It is required when the subject matter is new and/or highly specialized or technically complex. In a new field, for example regulating genetically modified crops, expert opinion may be required to develop criteria and judge whether they are being met. A variation of this method is an expert panel, in which more than one expert is consulted simultaneously. Unlike the expert opinion that is often qualitative, it is possible to quantify the information from an expert panel (WGEA, 2013: 60). This is usually required where the knowledge domain is highly contested. The WGEA water-related audit study found that expert opinion was used in about 25 per cent of cases (WGEA, 2013: 58), whereas an expert panel was used in less than 5 per cent of cases (WGEA, 2013: 60). In this book, no distinction has been made between expert opinion and the use of an expert panel.

Literature survey: This involves using the work of other studies and investigations and audits. Some audit issues, having a long history, may have several previously completed studies, often unpublished, such as consultant reports, internal audit and evaluation reports, or sometimes even publicly available works such as those of parliamentary/legislative committees, universities and voluntary organizations. Such material can provide useful information for audit planning and even as audit evidence (CAG, 2007: 13). This method is quite often used. For example, NAO uses literature survey in more than 45 per cent of its performance audits (Lonsdale, 2011b: 103).

Case study: A case study is a descriptive, exploratory or explanatory analysis of an organization, programme or project. The method is used to learn about a complex issue by developing a comprehensive understanding of the particular instance. It involves an extensive description and analysis of the particular issue within the context of the whole audit area. This method is also quite frequently used. Between 35–40 per cent use is reported in the literature (see, for example, Lonsdale, 2011b: 103; WGEA, 2013: 57).

Benchmarking: This involves comparing the performance of the activity, project, programme or organization being audited with the performance of a similar activity, project, programme or organization in other organizations or jurisdictions. Sometimes internal/national benchmarking is differentiated from international benchmarking (see, for example, Lonsdale, 2011b: 103; WGEA, 2013: 51), However, in this book no such differentiation has been made. This method is not very frequently used. For example, only 5–15 per cent use is reported (Lonsdale 2011b: 103; WGEA, 2013: 64).

Focus groups: Focus group involves a moderated discussion among a group of people – usually 7–12 individuals. Unlike an expert panel, the individuals are not experts, but stakeholders of the projects/programmes being audited. They meet for a specified period of time (generally face to face, but may also meet via the internet) to discuss programme implementation challenges or potential changes. This method is not yet very popular among SAIs. For example, WGEA (2013: 61) found it was used in just under 5 per cent of audits.

Specific economical/statistical analysis: This method involves monetary matters such as price comparison of alternative options to achieve an objective, and cost–benefit analysis of a project or programme that takes into account the opportunity cost of resources used and benefits accruing to the community or country as a whole. SAIs use this method to determine optimum use of resources. It is evident that it is a specialist type of analysis much beyond the usual graphing or tabulation of a project's or programme's numerical data. This method is used very infrequently. For example, the WGEA study (2013: 61) found it was used in less than 5 per cent of cases.

Scientific modelling (such as hydrological or ecological): This is a broad range of scientific analysis involving modelling such as hydrological and ecological models. WGEA (2013: 63) has also used this term to include analyses that demonstrate the cause–effect empirical relationship between programme goals and impact, as well as chemical testing. The term used in this book is in the sense of modelling only. For example, the use of remote sensing to determine farmed or forested area is considered as modelling.

References

ANAO. (2015). Performance Audit Manual. Melbourne: Australian National Audit Office.

CAG. (2007). *The Supplementary Guidelines: Evidence Gathering, Analysis and Evaluation Techniques in Performance Audit*. New Delhi: Comptroller and Auditor General of India.

INTOSAI. (2004). *Performance Audit Guidelines: ISSAI 3000–3100*. Stockholm: INTOSAI.

Lonsdale, J., Wilkins, P. & Ling, T. (2011a). *Performance Auditing: Contributing to Accountability in Democratic Government*. Cheltenham: Edward Elgar.

Lonsdale, J. (2011b). The right tools for the job? Methods, choice and context. In J. Lonsdale, P. Wilkins & T. Ling (Eds), *Performance Auditing: Contributing to Accountability in Democratic Government* (pp. 95–117). Cheltenham: Edward Elgar.

Pollitt, C., Girre, X., Lonsdale, J., Mul, R., Summa, H. & Waerness, M. (1999). *Performance or Compliance? Performance Audit and Public Management in Five Countries*. Oxford: Oxford University Press.

WGEA. (2013). *Auditing Water Issues: An Examination of SAIs' Experiences and the Methodological Tools They Have Successfully Used*. Stockholm: INTOSAI.

Index

Note: Page numbers in **bold** refer to tables and in *italics* to figures.